Historic
GLOUCESTER

AN ILLUSTRATED GUIDE TO
THE CITY, ITS BUILDINGS,
THE CATHEDRAL AND THE DOCKS

Historic
GLOUCESTER

AN ILLUSTRATED GUIDE TO
THE CITY, ITS BUILDINGS,
THE CATHEDRAL AND THE DOCKS

PHILIP MOSS

PUBLISHED IN ASSOCIATION WITH THE GLOUCESTER CIVIC TRUST AND
GLOUCESTER CITY COUNCIL

THE WINDRUSH PRESS · GLOUCESTERSHIRE

First published in Great Britain by
The Windrush Press
Little Window
High Street, Moreton-in-Marsh
Gloucestershire
1993

A percentage of the royalties from this book will be donated to the
Gloucester Civic Trust

Telephone: 0608 652012
Fax: 0608 652125

A catalogue record for this book is available in the British Library

ISBN 0 900075 28 7

Typeset by Carnegie Publishing Ltd., 18 Maynard Street, Preston, Lancs.

Printed and bound in Great Britain by The Cromwell Press Ltd., Melksham, Wilts.

The Author

Philip Moss was born in Gloucester and educated at the Crypt Grammar School, the Gloucester College of Art and the Royal West of England Academy of Art at Bristol where he studied illustration. He now works as a freelance illustrator and designer.

His interest in the city's history began in 1966 when he dug on the archaeological excavations in Bell Lane. As a founder member of the Gloucester and District Archaeological Research Group and as an active member of Gloucester Civic Trust since its inception in 1972 he has built up an extensive knowledge of his home city.

He is a Tourist Guide registered with the Heart of England Tourist Board and has assisted with the training of the Civic Trust's Guides since their formation in 1975

Acknowledgements

This book is the culmination of over twenty years interest in my native city and contains just a fraction of the history of Gloucester and its people.

I am indebted to Barbara Drake for her generosity in sharing the results of her research into the Westgate Street area, and similarly to Hugh Conway-Jones for the Docks area. I must also pay tribute to the late Arthur Dodd without whose friendship, wit and humour my search for Gloucester's history would have been less pleasurable. Thanks are also due to Nigel Spry and Robert Martin for reading various drafts of the text and providing valuable comments. Finally I must thank my wife Gillian for translating my sometimes illegible scribble onto computer disk.

To Gillian

Contents

Maps

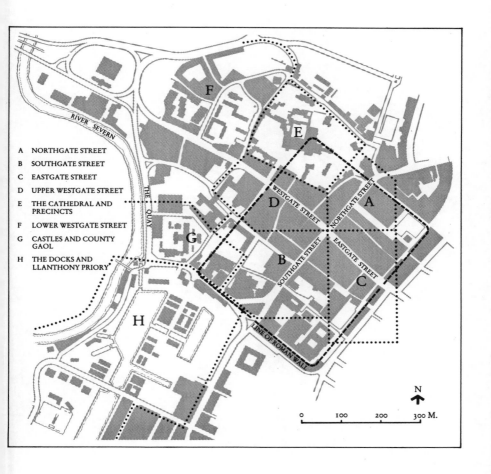

A NORTHGATE STREET
B SOUTHGATE STREET
C EASTGATE STREET
D UPPER WESTGATE STREET
E THE CATHEDRAL AND
  PRECINCTS
F LOWER WESTGATE STREET
G CASTLES AND COUNTY
  GAOL
H THE DOCKS AND
  LLANTHONY PRIORY

RIVER SEVERN

THE QUAY

WESTGATE STREET

NORTHGATE STREET

EASTGATE STREET

SOUTHGATE STREET

LINE OF ROMAN WALL

N

0   100   200   300 M.

An Outline History

GLOUCESTER HAS BEEN VARIOUSLY DESCRIBED as 'The Gateway to the West' and 'The Crossroads of England'. Certainly the importance of the site was realised in the late 40s or early 50s AD when the invading Roman army decided to build a fortress at Kingsholm near the lowest practicable crossing of the River Severn. This stronghold was eventually dismantled in the late 60s following the construction of a new fortress just to the south on the site of the present city centre. This became the springboard for the military advance into Wales. The army headquarters later moved to Caerleon leaving Gloucester behind the new western frontier as a settlement for time-expired legionary veterans. The urban life of Gloucester began with the community of traders and camp followers that grew around the military establishment and the city received its first charter during the reign of Emperor Nerva (AD 96–8) when it was granted the title of *Colonia Nervia Glevensis*. *Colonia* was the highest status a Roman provincial town could attain and was an administrative centre governed by a council and four magistrates. Glevum as it was more popularly known prospered and expanded and by the second century possessed a planned street layout with many imposing buildings, piped water supply and extensive suburbs. Since the early 1970s archaeological excavations have revealed the Roman North and East Gates, the Forum and Basilica and several private houses that afforded a luxurious lifestyle equal to any in Britain.

Following the departure of the Roman army in the fifth century there was little to stop the invading Anglo-Saxons reaching Gloucester and, according to the *Anglo-Saxon Chronicle*, a decisive battle was fought at Dyrham in 577 which ended with the slaying of three British kings, or chieftains, Conmail, Condidan and Farinmail and the capture of Gloucester, Cirencester and Bath. The Saxon victors, a subordinate tribe of the Mercian dynasty called the Hwicce settled in Gloucestershire and part of Worcestershire. In 679 Osric, king of the Hwicce, founded a monastery at Gloucester dedicated to St Peter on or near the site now occupied by the cathedral.

By the tenth century the town was an important part of the Kingdom of Mercia and had been re-fortified and re-planned by

Queen Aethelflaeda, daughter of Alfred the Great, against the incursions of the Danish armies from Brittany. The street plan of modern Gloucester is a direct legacy of this revitalisation. She also founded the New Minster church of St Oswald, c. 900, which became a national shrine following the installation of the bones of the seventh-century king and saint.

During the reign of Edward the Confessor the great hall of the Royal Manor or Palace at Kingsholm became the regular meeting place of the King and the Great Council – the Witanagemot – thus raising the status of Gloucester to that of Winchester and London.

In 1066 William of Normandy claimed the English throne and continued the practice of holding meetings of the Great Council at Gloucester. It was at one such gathering in 1085 that William I called for the detailed survey of his kingdom resulting in the production of the Domesday Book. The conqueror also had a profound effect on the religious life of Gloucester when he appointed Serlo of Bayeux, a Norman monk, to restore the flagging fortunes of the near defunct abbey of St Peter. Serlo began by building the great abbey church in the Norman style and the huge pillars of the nave are an important feature in the present cathedral. Perhaps the first Norman building to be imposed on the town was a motte and bailey castle. The 20m. (65 ft.) high mound was built in the south-west corner of the walled town and was topped with a timber tower with a defended enclosure – the bailey – on its east side. This together with the rebuilding of some of the town gates became a symbol of the king's authority over the indigenous Anglo-Saxon population. The timber and earth castle was replaced in the early twelfth century by a large stone keep, complete with surrounding walls and deep moat, just to the west on the east bank of the River Severn.

Gloucester's importance was confirmed under the Plantagenets by the grant of a charter by Henry I in 1155 which gave the town privileges equal to those of Westminster and London.

On 28 October 1216 the nine-year-old Henry III was led from the Royal Palace at Kingsholm to his coronation in St Peter's Abbey. He is the only English monarch since the Conquest to be crowned outside Westminster. Henry was a deeply religious man who did much for the church in Gloucester during his long reign. It was he who was responsible for the grants of oaks from the Royal Forest of Dean for the building of the Dominican and Franciscan Friaries in the town. Remains of both houses survive: Blackfriars – England's most complete Dominican Friary – dates from 1239 and Greyfriars from the rebuild of the early sixteenth century. The house of the Carmelites or

Whitefriars erected just outside the north-east corner of the town wall was similarly endowed but today, sadly, no trace remains. Henry's zeal for establishing religious houses was tempered by his political troubles. By a strange quirk of fate the city of his coronation became his prison when in 1263 Simon de Montfort held him captive in Gloucester Castle during the Barons' War.

Many significant parliaments were held at Gloucester in the following one and half centuries including one held by Henry IV in 1407 which paved the way for bringing public finances under parliamentary control.

The fortunes of medieval Gloucester were strengthened in 1327 when Abbot Thokey accepted for burial at St Peter's Abbey the body of King Edward II who was murdered at nearby Berkeley Castle. During the next two centuries many people were moved to make the pilgrimage to Edward's tomb, resulting in increased wealth and importance for the city and abbey. Craftsmen began restoring and beautifying the church and by the 1470s the building had reached its present size, complete with exquisite fan tracery in the cloisters and the glorious tower of Abbot Seabrooke. In this period other ancient city churches were also rebuilt and adorned with Perpendicular style towers.

In 1483 Richard III granted the charter on which the city's local government is largely based. It conferred on the burgesses of Gloucester the right of electing a mayor and twelve aldermen. To maintain the dignity of these new officers it also provided that the mayor should have a sword of state carried before him with two sergeants at mace to serve him.

King Henry VIII and his new wife Anne Boleyn visited Gloucester in July 1535 staying as guests of the abbot of St Peter's. It was in this same year that the Act of Supremacy was passed making Henry the Supreme Head of the Church of England and by 1536 the suppression of the smaller monasteries had commenced. By 1540 the dissolution of the larger monastic houses of Gloucester was well advanced and the episcopal see of Gloucester was established. The abbey church became the Cathedral of the new Diocese.

Henry VIII made England a protestant country, a policy which his son Edward VI continued, but Mary Tudor, his daughter, was determined to restore Roman Catholicism. So many protestant clergy were martyred during her reign that she acquired the nickname 'Bloody Mary'. During these persecutions Bishop John Hooper, the second Bishop of Gloucester, suffered martyrdom for his faith by being burnt at the stake in St Mary's Square on 9 February 1555.

Mary was succeeded by the protestant Elizabeth who granted Gloucester the status of a port in 1580. The city is said to be the most inland port in the country.

In 1642 civil war broke out in England. The cause of the war being Parliament's struggle against the absolute government of King Charles I, his alleged encouragement of popery and his illegal taxation. The strong growth of Puritanism in Gloucester from the late sixteenth century determined its support for the parliamentary cause. Within a year of the outbreak of war the parliamentary forces suffered many reverses and Gloucester alone stood against the king in the west. On 10 August 1643 a royalist army commanded by the king himself laid siege to the city. Gloucester was the only Roundhead garrison between the recently captured Bristol and the north-west, its capture would control the River Severn at its lowest crossing point.

The garrison in Gloucester was commanded by the 23-year-old Colonel Edward Massey. Under his command were two infantry regiments, 200 horse and dragoons and a few trained bands amounting to 1500 men. At the height of the siege the king had at his disposal a force of some 30,000 royalists. It says much for Massey and his puny garrison that with only the rather dubious protection of Gloucester's medieval town walls and some hastily thrown up earthworks the citizens resisted the artillery bombardment for 26 days. The king was forced to retreat on hearing that a relieving parliamentary army from London was nearing the city. 'Ever remember the fifth of September' was a motto adopted by Gloucestrians following the raising of the siege and this date became an annual holiday known as 'Gloucester Day'.

The eighteenth century saw the steady growth of Gloucester both in size and as a social centre. Local industry continued to flourish due to the proximity of iron-ore, coal and timber in the Forest of Dean. The city became renowned for pin manufacturing and the centuries old industry of bell founding continued apace. It has been said that many belfries in England contain at least one bell cast by the famous Rudhall family of Gloucester.

During the same century Robert Raikes, editor of the influential Gloucester Journal, established his Sunday School movement and George Whitefield the fiery evangelist began his ministry in the city. Sir George Onesiphorus Paul gave practical evidence to Parliament of his concern over prison reform by recommending the building of the present Gloucester Gaol which was, at the time, the finest and most advanced in the country.

Progress was accelerated during the early nineteenth century by the completion of the Gloucester and Sharpness canal in 1827 which resulted in the growth of the local timber industry. The waterway was then the longest, deepest and widest ship canal in Britain and afforded a direct route from Gloucester to the Scandinavian countries. The port facilities were expanded, including new dry docks and additional warehousing for the handling of grain. The coming of the railways in the 1840s also served to make the city more attractive to industry. In the Victorian era the city boundaries were extended, the population grew six-fold and many exuberant buildings were constructed.

The twentieth century witnessed the establishment of other notable industries such as aircraft production, railway rolling stock, motor cycles and match manufacturing. Although some of these firms are no longer trading, the city has maintained a diverse commercial and industrial base. This together with the important contribution that tourism makes to the local economy will ensure that the city continues to thrive.

Gloucester has undergone many changes in its long and eventful history but much of the old medieval city still remains and it is hoped that this book will help the reader to discover the 'Glories of Gloucester'.

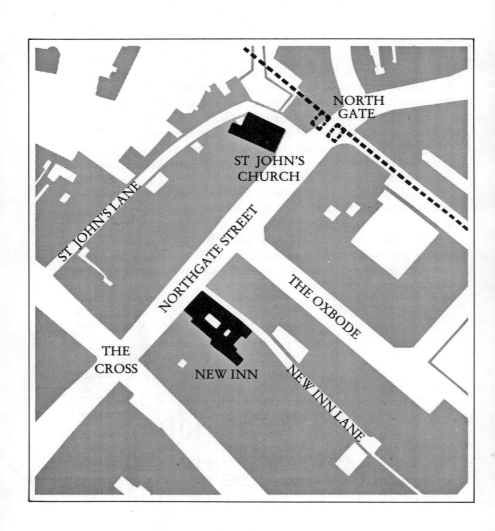

Northgate Street

The Cross

The meeting point of the four principal streets has been the focal point of Gloucester for nearly two thousand years. From the early thirteenth century this was marked by a large stone cross which, by 1455, also functioned as a conduit supplied with spring water piped in from Robinswood Hill 3.2 km. (2 miles) away. This octagonal structure was repaired and altered many times but by the late seventeenth century it had reached its ultimate size and form, standing over 10.3 metres (34½ ft.) high. Each face of the monument had acquired a large niche into which was set a lifesize carved stone figure of various sovereigns of England. It is thought that these statues originally belonged to a similar cross that stood in College Green and that they were removed at the time of its demolition in the 1640s. The High Cross of Gloucester was taken down in 1751 together with other obstructive buildings in the main streets 'for the better conveniency of carriages'.

Northgate Street

The North Gate was the main entrance to the city from London and the east. By the Middle Ages the street had become a principal trading area making it an ideal location for various markets. The earliest mention of the street by name occurs in 1342. By that time the cordwainers – or leatherworkers – had a well-established community at its south-western end manufacturing shoes, sword sheaths, belts and other goods. A permanent market house for meal – or flour – had been built by 1570 adjoining the east end of St John's Church. Local fruit produce and poultry were sold in other parts of the street by the early 1700s. On market days further congestion was caused by the establishment of the more pungent pig market held between Oxbode Lane and the gate.

The New Inn

The New Inn has been described as the finest example of a medieval galleried inn to be seen in Britain today. Much of the original structure remains together with its richly carved detail. Particularly interesting is the decapitated angel on the southern corner of the adjacent lane. The inn was originally built by St Peter's Abbey between 1430 and 1450 to accommodate the growing number of visitors to the city, and replaced an earlier inn on the site, thus acquiring the title 'New'.

John Twyning, the Town Monk, supervised the raising of the oak and chestnut timber frame buildings that enclosed two stone flagged courtyards. On completion it was held to be the largest inn in the country capable of catering for over two hundred persons at any one time, housed mostly in dormitory type accommodation. The medieval traveller often provided his own food to be cooked by the kitchen staff and the row of hooks in the ceiling of the south gallery, the coolest and airiest place, were used for the hanging and storage of meat.

The hostelry's ample accommodation was needed in 1553 when, at the city chamberlain's expense, a vast retinue of knights, gentlemen and yeomen lodged at Gloucester to proclaim the accession of Mary Tudor to the throne. Such announcements were usually made at the High Cross but during inclement weather the sheltered galleries of the inn would have provided an ideal substitute.

Throughout the centuries landlords have taken every opportunity to improve trade by providing entertainment and meeting facilities. During the sixteenth century it is said that plays were staged in the courtyard by travelling companies. At the end of the century a Puritan Conventicle gathered here regularly in the midst of a spirited campaign by the local magistrates to suppress alehouses and their attendant drunkenness! Gloucester's first recorded Real Tennis court was installed in the rear part of the building and by 1649 it had become a popular attraction for the more athletic citizens.

The second half of the eighteenth century saw the establishment of the New Inn as a noted venue for the unusual and bizarre. The enterprising landlord, Mr Nelson, sought to increase custom by providing facilities for the many travelling shows that passed through the city. Among the varied promotions he offered were Maria Theresa the 86 cm. (2 ft. 10 in.) tall Corsican Fairy, The Royal Family modelled lifesize in wax, a mermaid captured off the Mexican coast, exotic birds, and wild animal shows that included leopards, llamas, lions, tigers and hyenas. Each show could be viewed for the bargain price of 6d. (2½p).

With the advent of the motor car the courtyards of the Inn witnessed an interesting mix of both horse and horseless carriages. A few days before Christmas 1896 the Hon. C. S. Rolls, of Rolls Royce fame, set out on a journey from London to his parents' home in Monmouth. Travelling by way of Cirencester he elected to negotiate the steep descent of Birdlip Hill just to the east of Gloucester. On the steepest part of the hill the brakes failed on his open-topped Peugeot motor car and after careering downhill at breakneck speed the shaken Mr Rolls decided to stay the night at the New Inn. Next morning he repaired the faulty brakes but when he came to start up he did not realise that the car had been left in gear and as he swung the starting handle the engine fired and he had the humiliating experience of being run over by his own vehicle. Fortunately he was unhurt but was unable to prevent the car from ramming a dog-cart which the red-faced motorist had to repair before continuing his journey.

In the courtyard the lion and the serpent have been locked in combat since the middle of the nineteenth century representing the triumph of good over evil. Heraldic shields can be seen on and above the gallery. The shield with the three chevronels and ten torteaux is the older of the two and forms part of the present day city coat of arms. The chevronels are taken from the arms of the de Clare family who were Earls of Gloucester and the torteaux were derived from the arms of the see of Worcester which included Gloucester until 1541. The Tudor Coat was granted to the town in 1538 and is, heraldically

speaking, unusual but attractive. The roses are those of Lancaster and York, the boar's head is from the badge of Richard III, Duke of Gloucester, and the horseshoes and nails represent the important medieval ironworking industry in Gloucester. In 1647 the city corporation decided to revert to the older shield but the Tudor shield continued in popular use.

The New Inn remains a popular place for meetings and entertainment. Shakespeare's plays are occasionally performed here and the medieval setting provides an ideal venue for the regular appearances of the local mummers and morris dancers.

The Oxbode

The shopping thoroughfare was created in 1929 following the removal of Oxbode Lane together with its decaying and unwholesome dwellings. The ancient lane had a feature common to all alleyways and lanes in the city; as the lane approached the main street it became progressively narrower caused by the gradual encroachment of the Northgate Street properties with their commercially desirable frontages. Oxbode (pronounced Oxbody) Lane was said to be so narrow at this junction that an ox on its way to market became stuck fast between the buildings on either side. A local nursery rhyme relates how the animal was eventually removed steak by steak!

> There's an ox lying dead at the end of the lane,
> His head on the pathway, his feet in the drain,
> The lane is so narrow, his back was so wide,
> He got stuck in the road 'twixt a house on each side.
>
> He couldn't go forward, he couldn't go back,
> He was stuck just as tight as a nail in a crack,
> And the people all shouted, 'So tightly he fits
> We must kill him and carve him and move him in bits.'
>
> So a butcher despatched him and then had a sale
> Of his ribs and his sirloin, his rump and his tail;
> And the farmer he told me, 'I'll never again
> Drive cattle to market down Oxbode Lane.'

St John's Northgate

The earliest church on this site is reputed to have been founded in 931 by the Saxon King Athelstan who made it a Priory of Black Canons of St Augustine. Athelstan, the self-styled King of All England and favourite grandson of Alfred the Great, was a regular visitor to Gloucester and indeed died here in 940. In the eleventh century the church came into the possession of St Peter's Abbey and was rebuilt and dedicated to St John the Baptist. The medieval church measured 24.4 metres (80 ft.) long by 15.29 metres (50 ft.) wide and consisted of a large nave and south aisle, a chancel and a porch on the north side. The interior contained at least four chantries and three chapels dedicated to St Bridget, St Thomas and St Clement the Martyr. The latter was probably founded in the fifteenth century by the Fraternity of the Craft of Tanners whose common meeting or Guild Hall was in nearby Hare Lane.

There is little evidence of a sanctuary in this early church. However, following the slaying of Richard III, Duke of Gloucester, at Bosworth Field in 1485, three of his followers Francis Viscount Lovell, Lord Humphrey Stafford and his brother Thomas fled to Gloucester and sought refuge in St John's church in an effort to evade capture.

The parish of St John's was relatively well populated and included some of Gloucester's principal citizens; no fewer than seven mayors of the city were buried here. Among them the royalist Thomas Price who served Charles I as Master of Horse at the time of the civil war and who regained prominence in the city after the monarchy was restored in 1660. The elaborate memorial containing his effigy, raised following his death in 1678, can be seen on the north wall of the chancel.

By the early eighteenth century the fabric of the building had become delapidated and unsafe and by 1732 it had been demolished leaving only the fourteenth-century tower and steeple to be incorporated into its successor. The new church, opened in 1734, was built on the basilica plan with a nave and two aisles separated by an arcade of Doric columns with a rich classical façade onto Northgate Street.

The interior was fitted out with new seating, with only a few of the old pews being re-used. A three-decker pulpit was installed, now to be seen reduced to one stage. Both John Wesley and George Whitefield, the Gloucester born evangelist, preached from this pulpit, the former in 1739, the latter in 1741.

Many reminders of the old building were retained including a wooden parish chest of 1517 and a fine wrought iron swordrest dating from 1714 originally bearing the arms of George I which were altered to those of George II in 1727. The medieval font was re-cut and a quantity of grave slabs and memorials were reinstated, the most notable among them to Thomas Rich, founder of the Blue Coat School in Eastgate Street and Abel Rudhall of the famous family of Gloucester bell-founders. Others representing various trades and occupations in the parish can also be seen, mostly in the nave and north aisle.

The stained glass in the east window is a nineteenth-century memorial to Thomas Stock who was rector of St John's from 1787 until his death in 1803. Stock, together with his friend Robert Raikes, pioneered the development of schools on Sundays for the poor children of the city which culminated in the international Sunday School movement.

In 1972 the church was renamed St John's Northgate following a sharing agreement between the congregations of St John the Baptist and the nearby Northgate Methodist church, since demolished.

The North Gate

The remains of the Roman and medieval gates lie beneath the building on the north corner of St John's Lane and extend eastwards under the roadway. The medieval gate was one of the official entry points into the town used for the collection of tolls. This function was later transferred to the Outer North Gate which was built following the expansion of the city suburbs along lower Northgate Street. By 1520 the room over the gateway was in use as the main prison of the town and continued as such for well over two centuries but by 1780 conditions had become so cramped that prisoners were allowed to exercise on the roof.

Arrival at the North Gate following a long and possibly hazardous journey would have brought relief to the medieval traveller, perhaps in more ways than one. By the fourteenth century the authorities in Gloucester had provided public latrines at several entrances to the town. The one here was erected over the Fullbrook stream that ran immediately in front of the gateway before flowing westwards into the precincts of St Peter's Abbey. In 1372 the monks complained bitterly that the stench from this latrine was so foul that it prevented them from praying! The outrage had been caused by the watercourse apparently living up to its name.

The North Gate together with the Outer North and South Gates were demolished following an Act of Improvement of 1781.

Doctor Foster

> Doctor Foster
> Went to Gloucester
> In a shower of rain
> He stepped in a puddle
> Right up to his middle
> And never went there again.

The well-known nursery rhyme is generally held to be a comment upon the perilous state of Gloucester's roads in antiquity. It has been suggested that the verse refers to a visit by Edward I when his horse became immobilised after sinking deep into the mud of a city street. In consequence the king refused to visit Gloucester again.

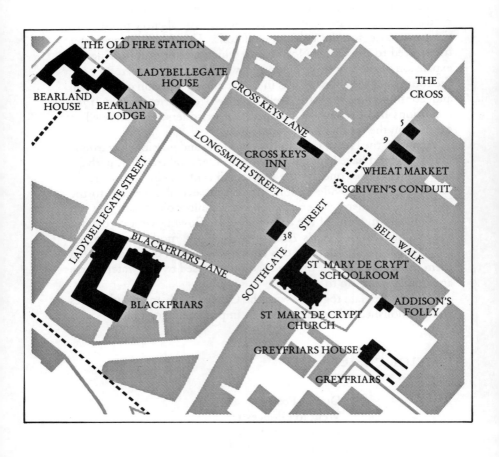

THE OLD FIRE STATION

LADYBELLEGATE
HOUSE

THE
CROSS

BEARLAND
HOUSE

BEARLAND
LODGE

CROSS KEYS LANE

5

9

CROSS KEYS
INN

LONGSMITH STREET

WHEAT MARKET

SCRIVEN'S CONDUIT

LADYBELLEGATE STREET

STREET

BELL WALK

38

BLACKFRIARS LANE

SOUTHGATE

ST MARY DE CRYPT
SCHOOLROOM

ADDISON'S
FOLLY

BLACKFRIARS

ST MARY DE CRYPT
CHURCH

GREYFRIARS HOUSE

GREYFRIARS

Southgate Street

Three metres (10 ft.) beneath the roadway and the buildings on either side lie the extensive remains of the Roman forum that stretch from the Cross to Bell Walk. The latter marks the centre line of the eastern half of the monumental basilica building that was the administrative centre for the town.

Southgate Street was created in the tenth century by cutting through the remnants of the forum to give access to the South Gate which opened onto the primary route to Bristol and the south-west. The street had acquired its present name by 1141 but later was often referred to as the Great South Street due to its prominence as a trading area. Fish sellers had established pitches near the Cross by the early thirteenth century and by 1509 a pillared market house for the sale of wheat had been built in the centre of the roadway opposite Cross Keys Lane. This was also the site of the medieval pillory where, on market days, lawbreakers were subjected to public humiliation by the towns-people who, no doubt, were able to obtain a plentiful supply of missiles from the various stalls nearby.

In 1636 the publicly spirited Alderman John Scriven built an elaborately carved conduit between the Wheat Market and Longsmith Street to serve the area with clean water from the supply piped in from Robinswood Hill. Previously the local inhabitants could only obtain water from a tap at the High Cross or from wells at the rear of their houses. The local well water was noted for its lively sparkling properties but this had more to do with the infusion of ammonia leaching from adjacent cess pits than the presence of any natural health giving minerals. Scriven's Conduit can be viewed today in Hillfield Gardens, London Road.

5 Southgate Street

The well-known Gloucester clock maker G. A. Baker began trading from an old medieval house on this site in 1882. The existing building dates from 1904. The fine Edwardian shopfront is surmounted by an unusual mechanical clock manufactured by Niehus Bros. of Bristol. It has five striking jacks or figures representing England, Ireland,

Scotland and Wales that sound the
chimes in the notes of A, B, D, and
G respectively with Father Time
striking the hours in D. In con-
sideration of nearby residents, the
chimes and strike remain silent
between 9 p.m. and 9 a.m.

9 Southgate Street

This interesting building with a Jacobean timber façade was originally
the mansion house of Thomas Yate, apothecary. On the first floor is
an elaborate fireplace with a richly detailed overmantel which bears
the date 1650. It also displays the family's coat of arms quartered with
those of Box and Berkeley. At the base of the overmantel are the
figures of four seated cherubs which, according to local tradition, are
said to represent the four sons of the original owner. Close inspection
will reveal that one of the cherubs has six fingers on one hand as did,
apparently, one of the young Yates.

The house is a prominent
feature of the street today but
during the late eighteenth
century it was an even more
unmistakable landmark. The
occupier at this time was
James Lee, a tobacconist and
'bluemaker' who advertised
his presence by painting the
whole of the façade in an eye-
catching shade of brilliant
blue!

The Old Blue Shop as it was affectionately known throughout the
county came into the possession of John Taylor who was an eminent
local grocer and brandy merchant. The family lived over the shop for
several generations and it was here in March 1826 that Henry Yates
Jones Taylor was born. HYJT as he was generally referred to became
a celebrated local historian who diligently recorded the unusual and
eccentric stories of the more elderly inhabitants of the city. These tales
were regularly published in the local newspaper thus providing a
fascinating insight into the society of late eighteenth- and early
nineteenth-century Gloucester.

At the turn of the century the building was occupied by Mr Clark, tea merchant, who endeavoured to promote his choice stock of products from India and Ceylon by erecting a large fascia board which announced in lettering two feet high that here was 'THE CITY TEA WAREHOUSE'. This together with an enormous metal tea cannister set upon the parapet ensured that the house was once again the centre of attraction in Southgate Street. The upper floors eventually became redundant as living accommodation in 1912 and were leased to the historic Bell Hotel next door and put to use as meeting and function rooms. Sadly the Bell was torn down in 1969 leaving number 9 as a faint echo of that great establishment.

The Bell Inn

By the first half of the sixteenth century this famous inn had established itself as one of the finest hostelries in the city. Catering for the needs of travellers and locals alike it became the focus of eighteenth-century society. Weekly assemblies for the county gentry had become popular by the 1740s and the house was usually the chosen venue of leading academics and medical men when travelling the country demonstrating the latest advances in science. In 1785 the inn was appointed as the official stopping point for the London Mail Coach in addition to the long established Bristol and Bath stagecoaches. The Concert Room featured the latest music of the day and any performance of Handel's works proved very popular with the musically minded Gloucestrians. The Bell Inn was immortalised by Henry Fielding in his satirical novel *Tom Jones* published in 1749. In this he recommends the fayre and hospitality available and extols the virtues of Elizabeth, wife of landlord Richard Whitefield. Perhaps the most significant event to take place at the inn was the birth of Richard's youngest brother George, who achieved fame as one of the foremost evangelists of the eighteenth century.

George Whitefield

George Whitefield was born on 16 December 1714 at the Bell Inn where his father, Thomas, was licensee. Two years after his birth his father died leaving his wife to run the inn and look after seven children of whom George was the youngest. Mrs Whitefield was determined to see that he received a good education, first sending him to the King's School and later to the nearby Crypt School. Whitefield was not an outstanding pupil and was given to truancy but he showed great ability as an actor. On leaving school he became pot boy at his mother's inn, washing the mops and cleaning the rooms. However with the help of wealthier relatives he soon found his way to Pembroke College, Oxford, where he matriculated in 1732.

It was at Oxford that he first met John and Charles Wesley and in 1735 he joined their Christian society of students or 'Holy Club' whose members were referred to as 'Methodists'. Whitefield gradually drew away from the Wesleys in pursuit of his own religious fulfilment, but his health soon deteriorated through lack of regular nourishment and by praying out of doors in freezing weather in the fervent belief that the body should be subservient to the soul. Following his recovery at home in Gloucester he was ordained a deacon in 1736 and preached his first sermon in St Mary de Crypt church. The pulpit which he used, together with its sounding board, can still be seen in the nave. It has been said that fifteen people in the congregation went 'quite mad' with religious fervour. The Bishop, rather drily, observed that he 'hoped the madness would last'. Shortly after his ordination Whitefield went to London where he preached to capacity congregations that were generally drawn from the poorer classes. In the same year he preached for eight weeks in Hampshire followed by a tour of the west of England.

The 1730s saw the colonisation of Georgia, Britain's last American colony, and it was felt that the colonists were in need of spiritual guidance. George Whitefield proposed himself as a missionary but was unable to get a passage for nearly a year. During the intervening time he maintained a hectic schedule moving about the countryside as a gospel rover, preaching for the first time in the open air at Stonehouse, near Stroud. He eventually sailed to America early in 1738 returning later the same year.

He was ordained a priest in January 1739 but the Church of England pulpits were denied to him as a result of his connection with Dissenters. In order to overcome this he had a portable pulpit constructed for use in the open air. In August 1739 he was publicly denounced by the Bishop of London and shortly afterwards returned to America where he preached to large audiences from Pennsylvania in the north to Georgia in the south.

In 1741 Whitefield married Elizabeth James, a widow from Abergavenny, but is said to have been unhappy with the union; indeed, one biographer even went as far as to say that 'her death set his mind much at liberty'.

The impact of Whitefield on both English and American society was immense. He was an accomplished performer of no mean ability and his gestures were said to be natural and effective; but his greatest asset was his magnificent voice. Benjamin Franklin calculated that he could be heard by 30,000 people at any one time. As a child he had suffered from a bad attack of measles which left him with a distinct cast in his left eye. It was maliciously reported that each member of his congregation felt that he was being personally addressed since nobody could miss both eyes at once! He was even caricatured on the London Stage as 'Dr Squintum'.

Among his vast following of enthusiastic supporters was Selina, Countess of Huntingdon who during her lifetime built or acquired over sixty chapels.

In total Whitefield made seven voyages to America where he was ever mindful of the need to establish centres of learning. The Charity School he founded at Pennsylvania was the forerunner of the present University and he was also involved in the creation of the college at Princeton, New Jersey. In fact no fewer than fifty-one American schools or colleges owe their inception to him. During his sixth visit to the colonies the library of Harvard University was totally destroyed by fire and it was Whitefield who secured a large gift of books from England to re-equip the new building.

He died on Sunday 30 September 1777 at Newburyport, Massachusetts, having preached no fewer than 18,000 sermons to an estimated 10 million people in his lifetime.

Cross Keys Lane

The street takes its present name from the sixteenth-century timber-framed inn that stands on the south side. Prior to the Reformation the sign of the Cross Keys usually meant an inn that was supplied with wine and beer from a nearby monastic house. The sign is also the emblem of Saint Peter who was patron saint of Gloucester Abbey.

In the medieval period the street was known as Scroddelone or Scrud Lane – derived from the Anglo-Saxon word *Scrud*, meaning shroud or garment. It was a common practice to identify a thoroughfare by the trades carried on within it, and this site was occupied by clothiers workshops in the tenth century.

Bell Walk

Formerly Bell, or Bellmans Lane commemorating the site of William Henshawe's bell foundry which operated here in the sixteenth century.

Longsmith Street

The name of this street recalls one of the most important industries within the medieval town, for here was the centre of iron production. Quality iron was produced in the reign of Edward the Confessor and by the twelfth century the chronicler Geraldus Cambrensis commented that Gloucester had become famous for its ironworks and smithies.

Iron ore was obtained from nearby Robinswood Hill but the main source was the Forest of Dean, carried by water from inlets on the River Severn to Gloucester Quay.

All manner of goods were manufactured including the mattocks, spades, arrows and kitchen utensils that were ordered by King Henry II for his expedition to Ireland in 1173. Other products were also despatched to every part of Britain and France and to the Holy Land at the time of the crusades. In 1242 King Henry III placed an urgent order for 10,000 horseshoes and 100,000 nails to be delivered to Portsmouth in just twenty days which, no doubt, ensured a great deal of overtime in 'the street of the smiths'. Gloucester Castle was a regular customer during times of unrest and many smiths were employed to make crossbow bolts to restock the garrison's arsenal. Not all the products were of a warlike nature; iron pins, cramps and large quantities of nails were supplied for the fixing of stone and timber at the royal building works at Bedford, Windsor and Westminster.

Apart from the manufacture of raw iron many associated trades flourished, including locksmiths, cutlers, shieldmakers, knifesmiths and combmakers. The street had assumed its present name by 1549 but had previously been called Old Smith Street and Schoolhouse Lane, a school being recorded here as early as 1199. In the early eighteenth century its name changed temporarily to Bolt Lane, taken from an inn which presumably commemorated the fabrication of crossbow bolts on the site. But by this time the industrial activity of the area had long ceased and Longsmith Street had become a fashionable residential area.

Ladybellegate House

Ladybellegate House is arguably the finest town house in Gloucester. The tall façade is constructed of brick with quoins and other dressings of Cotswold stone. It originally had a pediment above the parapet and a slate roof surmounted by a cupola.

It was built about 1704 by Henry Wagstaffe on land first leased to his grandfather Edward, a wealthy brewer, in 1639. Their family fortunes had expanded following an Act of 1661 that removed from civic office those who had been disloyal to the king during the civil war.

Henry's father John, a royalist sympathiser, was nominated to the city council in 1662, later becoming an alderman and mayor in 1669 and 1678. He also represented the city in parliament from 1685–7. After his father's death in 1697 Henry took over the property and oversaw the rebuilding of the family town house in a style befitting someone who was to represent the county as sheriff in 1708. Henry died in 1725 and his widow Margaret continued to live at Ladybellegate House despite the considerable debts he left which eventually forced her to let the property to Robert Raikes the elder and to apprentice her two sons to tradesmen.

Robert Raikes first published the *Gloucester Journal* from an office in Northgate Street on 9 April 1722. The *Journal* soon established itself as a leading provincial newspaper of the eighteenth century, serving not only Gloucestershire but all of the surrounding counties and South Wales. In 1736 the first of five sons was born to Raikes and his third wife Mary. Robert the younger was destined to become nationally known as a compaigner for prison reform and a pioneer of the Sunday School movement. Other sons also led very distinguished lives. William was a noted merchant and director of the South Sea Company and Thomas, a close friend of Pitt the Younger, entered the world of finance and was later appointed Governor of the Bank of England. The Raikes family continued to live at Ladybellegate House until 1772 except for the years 1740–3 when it was leased to Henry Guise a member of the well-known county family of Elmore.

The house interior contains some of the city's most impressive eighteenth-century ornamental plasterwork. The ceiling of the pan-elled reception hall is decorated with a fine central rosette together with renderings of Greek philosophers' heads, and the spectacular ceiling in the main front room features female heads and deities in low relief. These two ceilings date from 1740, as does the one on the first floor landing that contains the Guise crest set into the border at each corner. The huge cloud-borne figure of Jupiter that glowers down from the staircase ceiling and the ornamental chimney pieces down-stairs are in the earlier baroque style and were probably installed by the original owner Henry Wagstaffe.

During the nineteenth century the Gloucester Liberal Club was founded at Ladybellegate House and by 1890 The Gloucester Friendly Societies' Medical Association retained the services of a doctor and established a dispensary here. More recently the building was used as a Health Centre with flats on the upper floor. Prior to the construction of the adjacent telephone exchange, it was purchased by Post Office Telephones who in turn sold the property to Gloucester Civic Trust for just £1. Following a successful restoration, the build-ing was officially re-opened by HRH The Princess Anne in 1979.

Robert Raikes the Younger

Robert and Mary Raikes' eldest son was born in
September 1736 and baptised at St Mary de
Crypt church. Initially he was educated at
the Crypt School and later at the Kings
School where he received a good grounding
in English, Latin and Greek. On leaving
school he was apprenticed to his father
who was the highly respected printer and
publisher of the *Gloucester Journal*.
Robert Raikes the elder died in 1757, aged
sixty-eight, leaving his widow to manage
the printing and stationery business until
his son attained his twenty-fifth birthday.
Quite soon after taking over the editorship, the
young Raikes made several changes to the newspaper
by enlarging the sheet size and improving the layout. Sharing his
father's concern over the need for prison reform, the columns of the
Journal were used to inform the public of the appalling conditions
that he witnessed in Gloucester Gaol in the role of a prison visitor.
The gaol had been particularly full following the riots of the 1760s
when many half-starved protestors were arrested for violently demonstrating against the high price of corn.

Robert Raikes married Anne Trigge of Newnham on 23 December
1767 at St James church, Picadilly, London. Returning to the family
home in Ladybellegate House they established a household of some
style in which they brought up their six daughters and two sons.

Raikes was described by a contemporary as a somewhat portly man
of medium weight with a fair complexion, who wore extravagant
fashionable attire topped out with a brown wig and three cornered
hat. He was also an inveterate taker of snuff which on special occasions
was elegantly dispensed from a large gold box. The diarist, Fanny
Burney, following a visit to his house, noted that Mr Raikes was
'somewhat too flourishing, somewhat too forward, somewhat too
voluble, but he is witty, benevolent, good natured and good hearted'
and that 'he kept a manservant and three maidservants' and was 'a
good liberal master who paid good wages.'

It was in the capacity of prospective employer that an incident
occurred which was to influence Raikes in the years ahead. On seeking

the services of a gardener he found himself in St Catherine Street in the northern suburbs of the city, where he was concerned to see a group of poor ragged children playing in the street. The gardener's wife replied that it was even worse on Sundays when the street was full of children cursing and swearing and spending their time in noise and riot. The children in question were mainly employed in the pin-making factories, working long hours for six days a week. Consequently, their pent up energy and frustration was given free rein on their day off. Raikes realised that the gaols were full of unfortunate people whose lives had been shaped by such deprivation in childhood.

The decision to establish schools on Sundays for these wretched children was taken soon afterwards following a discussion with the Rev. Thomas Stock, Rector of St John the Baptist Church. Suitable ladies were recruited at 1s. 6d. (7½p) a day to run the various schools, each of which came under the direct supervision of either Stock or Raikes. One of the first to be opened was at Mrs King's home in St Catherine Street where children between the ages of five and fourteen years were admitted regardless of the state of their clothes or demeanour. Lessons began at 10 a.m. until noon, resumed at 1 p.m. and continued until 5.30 p.m., the latter session including a reading lesson and a visit to church.

In spite of his good nature Robert Raikes could be both strict and stern, punishment was meted out for bad behaviour and in particular for telling lies. Rewards were given as an incentive to learning and good appearance; combs were regularly dispensed in an attempt to train even the most tousled head. There was also the Sunday School treat for the children who were occasionally invited to his house to receive lavish portions of Mrs Raikes' home-made plum cake.

The *Gloucester Journal* regularly reported the success and expansion of the movement throughout Britain which led John Wesley to remark 'I find these schools springing up wherever I go'. Suitable publications for use in the schools were advertised and Raikes himself produced, in 1785, a slim volume entitled *The Sunday School Companion*.

Robert Raikes, by then living in a house in Bell Lane, retired in 1802 and sold the newspaper to the printers of the *Hereford Times*. He spent his remaining years telling stories and teaching children to read and sing. On 5 April 1811 Raikes died suddenly of a heart attack at his home. His beloved school children attended his burial in St Mary de Crypt church and in compliance with his wishes they each received one shilling (5p) and a large plum cake.

Bearland Lodge

A very attractive early eighteenth-century house with an interesting pediment above the façade. It contains the half-lifesize figure of Minerva (Pallas Athene) in full relief with the head of the vanquished gorgon on her shield. The pediment sits a little uncomfortably into the design of the building and is almost certainly a later addition. It probably originated from nearby Ladybellegate House where the staircase ceiling features the figure of Jupiter. Minerva was the daughter of Jupiter who sprang from a hole in the top of his head following unorthodox treatment for a headache administered by his son Vulcan.

Bearland House

The house was built in the 1740s by William Jones, a distinguished Gloucester attorney. The ornamental façade is complemented by a forecourt enclosed by an east wing and fine wrought iron railings and gates. A similar wing to the west was removed early in the twentieth century.

Among the notable owners of the property was Samuel Hayward, JP, County High Sheriff, who purchased it in 1764 together with the land as far as Commercial Road to the south, and from Ladybellegate Street to Barbican Road in the west. Following Hayward's death the house was inherited by his daughter Catherine who continued to live here for many years. It is alleged that her white-clad figure still haunts the building, gazing out of the staircase window over what were once the formal gardens and orchards.

From the middle of the nineteenth century these extensive gardens gradually disappeared under development and the house was put to many uses apart from the purely domestic. In 1856 it became the depot for the local militia and a Post and Telegraph Office was built nearby in 1870. The whole of the Bearland estate was finally sold in 1899 to the Gloucester Corporation who constructed the City Electricity Works in 1900 on land bordering Commercial Road. The Girls Endowed School, later to become the Girls High School, Denmark Road, occupied the building for five years from 1904, succeeded by a firm of solicitors. In 1915 the Post Office Telephone Service centralised its Gloucester Area Headquarters here, remaining for the next fifty-five years.

In 1978 the building was purchased by the Preece Payne architectural practice who undertook a sympathetic restoration of the structure and its period fittings.

Bearland

An old Gloucester nursery rhyme recalls the story of a wandering bear, who, somewhat disgruntled at being unable to find a place to live, came to the city and carried off the mayor in protest. The citizens decided to placate the enraged creature by providing an area in the city just for bears, thus ensuring the return of their first citizen.

The truth, however, is much more mundane. The original name was 'bare land' referring to the open space that surrounded Gloucester Castle which gave the defending garrison a clear field of fire at any would-be besiegers.

In the medieval period the area was also known as 'Colstall' which means charcoal, vast quantities of which were consumed in the hearths of the Longsmith Street iron works.

The Old Fire Station

The station was officially opened in 1913 to house a newly-created city brigade. It remained the centre of fire control operations until 1956 when the function was transferred to a new station in Eastern Avenue.

Devastating fires occurred in Gloucester during the late twelfth and early thirteenth centuries. One in particular, in 1223, consumed the whole of the west side of Northgate Street and both sides of Westgate Street as far down as College Street. In a town built largely of timber the authorities were ever mindful of the need to provide equipment to tackle an outbreak of fire. Fire buckets were kept in various parish churches and fire hooks and chains for pulling down buildings were stored at the Barley Market in Eastgate Street. In 1648 the city's first mechanical fire engine was purchased from a London manufacturer at a cost of £30. This, together with the gradual replacement of timber framed buildings with the more fire resistant brick dwellings, seems to have prevented a repetition of the disastrous conflagrations of earlier centuries.

In the nineteenth century additional fire engines were provided by the Norwich Union and the Liverpool, London and Globe insurance companies who attended incidents at the appropriately marked premises. These private horse-drawn brigades were disbanded in 1912 following the formation of a new city brigade, an event that was marked by a farewell celebration dinner held at the New Inn in May of that year. Two months later a fire totally destroyed a furniture factory in the city. Unfortunately, the brigade's new motorised fire engine was out of commission with gearbox trouble!

In 1977 the ground floor of the Old Fire Station was adapted to house part of the City Museum's collection of wheeled vehicles.

38 Southgate Street: Robert Raikes House.

A fine sixteenth-century building with a decorative timber-framed façade and octagonal brick chimney stacks. The three gables have unusual carved barge boards that take their inspiration from the shape of yokes. At first floor level hang three sugar loaves, a traditional sign

for a grocer, suspended from a cast iron bracket that bears an inscription commemorating the building's connection with Robert Raikes the younger.

By the eighteenth century the property had been divided into two separate units; the 'best house' occupied the area beneath the middle and southern gables and the 'other house' beneath the northern one. Raikes moved the *Gloucester Journal* printing office into the former in 1758 transferring it from nearby Blackfriars. Following his marriage and subsequent occupation of the family home in Ladybellegate House, his mother, Mary, moved to the 'other house' in 1768 for the remaining eleven years of her life.

The Old Crypt Schoolroom

The façade onto Southgate Street has a facing of stone with mullioned windows restored in the nineteenth century, the rear elevation is constructed of Tudor brickwork with limestone buttresses and windows. The archway that spans the ancient thoroughfare of Marylone has the arms of King Henry VIII set above it together with shields featuring the Crypt School crest and the Tudor arms of the city.

Until early in the sixteenth century education in Gloucester was the sole prerogative of the Prior and monks of Llanthony Priory who, by the end of the twelfth century, had established a fee-paying school in Longsmith Street, near the junction of Bull Lane.

A successful attempt to break this monopoly was made in the 1520s by John Cooke, a wealthy mercer, who intended to create a school that offered free education to the young citizens of the city. Cooke, twice City High Sheriff and four times Mayor, unfortunately died in September 1528 before realising this worthy ambition, but left provision in his will for the work to proceed under the direction of his widow, Joan.

The schoolhouse was built on part of a burial ground purchased from Richard Hart, Prior of Llanthony and patron of St Mary de Crypt church, who stipulated that the rector of the parish should receive an annual payment of one red rose as part of the agreement, thus creating a tradition that survives to this day. The Crypt School opened in 1539 and continued on this site until 1861 when it moved to Barton Street, later transferring to Friars Orchard. In 1943 a new building was opened at Podsmead, built on land purchased by Dame Joan Cooke in 1539 as part of an endowment for maintaining the original school.

St Mary de Crypt Church

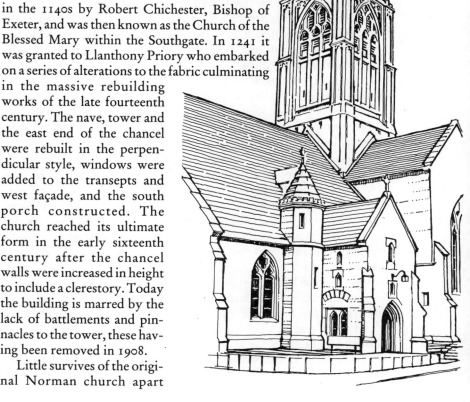

The earliest recorded church on this site was held in the 1140s by Robert Chichester, Bishop of Exeter, and was then known as the Church of the Blessed Mary within the Southgate. In 1241 it was granted to Llanthony Priory who embarked on a series of alterations to the fabric culminating in the massive rebuilding works of the late fourteenth century. The nave, tower and the east end of the chancel were rebuilt in the perpendicular style, windows were added to the transepts and west façade, and the south porch constructed. The church reached its ultimate form in the early sixteenth century after the chancel walls were increased in height to include a clerestory. Today the building is marred by the lack of battlements and pinnacles to the tower, these having been removed in 1908.

Little survives of the original Norman church apart

from some arches in a blocked-up portion of the crypt. This space below the west end of the nave has been put to some interesting and unusual uses. In the medieval period the crypt may have been used as a charnel house containing bones of the dead, but by 1576 it was occupied by living parishioners following its conversion into a tavern! This use continued for nearly one hundred years, apart from a short period when it was used as a timber store during the Siege of Gloucester in 1643. The church had been appropriated by the city corporation who turned it into an explosives manufactory and ammunitions store for the defending garrison; because of this function the building received a certain amount of attention from the royalist artillery just outside the city walls. The sundial set into the south-east buttress of the chancel is said to mark the point of impact of a cannon shot.

The fifteenth-century NAVE contains an early Renaissance-style pulpit from which George Whitefield preached his first sermon in 1736. In 1973 the space below the tower was re-ordered to accommodate a seventeenth-century communion table. Nearby is a wrought-iron mace rest used by the Mayor and Corporation in the reign of George II. High in the SOUTH AISLE at the eastern end is a carved stone head set into the wall, which, according to local tradition is of Henry Dene, Prior of Llanthony 1461–96, patron of the church and later archbishop of Canterbury.

In the NORTH TRANSEPT and NORTH AISLE are interesting sixteenth-century brasses to Alderman John Cooke and his wife Joan, founders of the adjacent Crypt School and to William Henshawe, bell-founder and five times mayor between 1503 and 1519, and each of his two wives, Alice and Agnes.

A stone screen dating from the 1920s encloses the NORTH CHAPEL that houses the kneeling effigy of Daniel Lysons who died 1681, the bust of Mayor Richard Lane, 1667, together with other church memorabilia.

The slender early eighteenth-century font was used to baptize George Whitefield and Robert Raikes who lies buried beneath the floor of the SOUTH CHAPEL that was dedicated to his memory in 1945. The chapel also contains the tomb chest of Sir Thomas and Lady Bell, notable worthies of the city, together with a recessed monument thought to be to Richard Manchester who provided funds for the first ring of five bells to be hung in the central tower in the fifteenth century. Today the tower contains a ring of eight bells, several of which were cast in the city during the eighteenth century by the Rudhall family.

Henry Dene is credited with carrying out various embellishments to the CHANCEL and the unusual single stone seat, or sedile, against the north wall is said to have been made for his own use. The more usual triple sedilia arrangement with their very fine canopies can be seen on the opposite wall. The ceiling was decorated with carved wooden bosses and angels playing musical instruments following the raising of the roof height and the installation of clerestory windows in the sixteenth century.

The tall Perpendicular east window houses a copy of medieval glass made by Rogers of Worcester in 1857. Below it is a Caen stone reredos decorated with venetian mosaics.

High on the eastern part of the NORTH WALL are remnants of an elaborate wall painting that was fully revealed in 1982. The subject is the Adoration of the Magi painted in oils directly onto the stonework, and is datable to the 1520s by the Flemish-style costume and architectural details. The three kings, Melchior, Balhazar and Caspar are depicted presenting gifts to the infant Jesus with Mary and Joseph looking on. The small figure waving to the onlooker from the top of the painting is thought to be a self portrait of the artist. On the opposite wall is another contemporary wall painting but the remains are so fragmentary that the subject remains obscure.

Greyfriars

The house of the Franciscan Friars was founded in Gloucester in 1231 on land given by Thomas, Lord Berkeley. King Henry III was also a major benefactor providing oak trees from the royal forests for the roofs and other timber work.

Initiates into the Franciscan order were required to take vows of poverty, chastity and obedience, but it seems that only poverty was absolute. The rules also forbade any form of decoration or embellishment within the house and one friar was disciplined for attempting to brighten up his new surroundings by 'painting the pulpit.' As punishment he was 'deprived of his hood' and the warden received similar treatment for tolerating pictures.

Twenty-four friars were in residence by 1277, rising to forty by 1284. The following year saw the start of a series of quarrels between the friars and the monks of St Peter's Abbey. It was alleged that the monks had forcibly taken away a body intended for burial at Greyfriars, no doubt coveting a sizeable burial fee in the process. Relations between the two religious houses were further strained in the fourteenth century following a clash over the shared water supply that was piped in from Robinswood Hill. The Abbey had somehow managed to appropriate most of the flow and the friars were described as being 'in want of water.' This acrimonious dispute was finally resolved by Edward the Black Prince during a visit to Gloucester when he granted the rights of the water to the Franciscans.

The church was rebuilt about 1518 at the expense of Maurice, Lord Berkeley and the standing remains date from this time. The NAVE and NORTH AISLE are of equal height and similar width and have no parallel in English mendicant orders, although examples of this layout can be found in France and Germany. The walls are decorated with blind panelling between and below the remaining four-light traceried windows. The shields on the exterior of the south wall of the nave display the arms of the Chandos and Clifford families and probably derive from a funerary monument.

Only five friars occupied the newly built house when it was sold following the dissolution in 1538. The church was immediately turned into a brewery that took advantage of the plentiful supply of fresh water.

The structure suffered severe damage from artillery fire during the siege of 1643 and, by 1721, the chancel together with the cloisters on the south side of the church had completely disappeared. The remains were sub-divided into dwellings that, in the nineteenth century, were occupied by the apothecary to the Gloucester Dispensary, a lodging house for sailors, and ultimately a wine and spirit merchant. These later additions were removed in the 1960s when the monument was taken into care by the Ministry of Works.

Greyfriars House

This three-storey house is set into the western end of the nave and north aisle of the Franciscan church. Built in 1810 for Philo Maddy, a Gloucester currier (a dealer in leather), it consists of a stone façade with a central pediment and a portico with Doric columns. It replaced an earlier house of the same name that was owned by Sir John Powell who represented the city in Parliament in 1685. Powell, a barrister,

served as town clerk in Gloucester for fifteen years at the end of the seventeenth century and was appointed to the bench in 1686, knighted in 1687 and ultimately served on the Queen's Bench from 1702. During his time as a judge the laws relating to witchcraft had not been repealed, although the voracity for witch hunting had abated. Jane Wenman had been taken into custody following sworn statements from her adversaries that she could fly. When brought before the judge he enquired whether the allegations were true. She replied that she could indeed fly, whereupon Powell immediately dismissed the case, ruling that there was no law against flying!

A contemporary described John Powell as 'the merriest old gentleman I ever saw, spoke pleasing things and chuckled till he cried.' He died in 1713 and is commemorated by his lifesize effigy in the Lady Chapel of Gloucester Cathedral.

Addison's Folly

Built in 1864 as a memorial to Robert Raikes by Thomas Fenn Addison, a solicitor, who lived in nearby Bell Lane. The tower was built high enough to afford Addison a view of Hempsted church, 2.4 km. (1½ miles) away to the southwest, where his wife Hannah was buried.

Blackfriars

The Dominican or Black Friars order was founded in 1217 by St Dominic and first arrived in England in 1221. The Friars Preachers were essentially teachers and evangelists, either travelling alone about the countryside or living communally in urban friaries. The Gloucester Black Friars was founded in 1239 by Sir Stephen, Lord of Harnhill, on a site that had once been part of the bailey of the Norman castle. King Henry III became a major benefactor of the friary, granting timber for the roofs, not only from the nearby Forest of Dean but also from royal forests in Shropshire and Dorset.

In accordance with their role as teachers, the friars at Gloucester had the distinction of establishing the first purpose-built library in England with which to maintain their zeal for learning.

The friary prospered through the next two centuries despite a series of scandals relating to the indiscipline of the brethren; William of

Hasfield, for instance, was severely censured in the 1330s for discard-
ing his habit and wandering about in a vagabond manner. The Do-
minicans acted as confessors to many important people, who in turn
bestowed generous gifts on the friary in which many of them would
ultimately be laid to rest. The site of the cemetery was confirmed in
1991 by an archaeological excavation just to the north of Blackfriars
Lane where no fewer than 140 burials were uncovered in an area
measuring just 20 x 2.5 metres (65½ x 8 ft.). Surprisingly the remains
of a number of women and children were discovered, indicating that
the Black Friars may have been operating a hospital or hospice for the
families of benefactors. It has been estimated that up to 1500 people
still lie buried within the medieval precincts of the friary.

The house was in decline by the early sixteenth century with the
former complement of between thirty and forty friars reduced to a
prior and six brethren living in extreme poverty at the time of the
Dissolution.

In 1539 Sir Thomas Bell, a wealthy Gloucester capper and clothier,
purchased the property for £240.5s.4d. (£240.28) and set about re-
modelling the church into a private dwelling house with other buildings being converted into a cloth manufactory providing employment
for over 300 townspeople. Access to the property was gained via two
gateways, one on Southgate Street and one on Longsmith Street, both
of which were referred to as Lady Bell's Gate after Thomas' wife,

Joan. Bell died in 1566 followed by his wife a year later; the property
then passed into the hands of the Dennis family who held it until the
late seventeenth century. Part of the cloistral ranges were turned into
dwellings in the eighteenth century and other buildings housed a
woolstapler and a stonemason's workshop. The great hall was leased
to an independent church in 1780 and, by the early nineteenth century,
a private school had been established here. By the 1930s Bell's mansion
had been divided into two separate houses and other tenants of the site
included a printing firm and a mineral water manufacturer. Restoration
of this, the finest surviving example of a Dominican Friary in Britain,
began about 1960 under the direction of the Ministry of Works.

The buildings of the Gloucester Black Friars are ranged in a
quadrangular plan around a COURTYARD measuring some 24.4m. (80
ft.) square enclosed by the church on the north side. The NAVE of the
church was specifically designed for use as a preaching place by friars
who delivered orations from a pulpit or lectern that probably stood
upon the rectangular stone base set into the centre of the floor. In the
fourteenth century NORTH and SOUTH TRANSEPTS were added to the
eastern end of the nave together with a timber steeple or lantern placed
above the centre of the crossing. The crowning glory of the church is
to be found in the ROOF structure formed by a series of individual
trusses of the collar beam and scissor-brace type. Similar construction
can be found in the east and south ranges, and it is remarkable how
well-preserved these thirteenth-century timbers remain. The western
end of the nave was shortened in the sixteenth century by Sir Thomas
Bell during the conversion of the church into a mansion which also
necessitated the removal of the narrow side aisles and the installation
of new floors, windows and fireplaces. The fireplace set into the
rebuilt WEST WALL probably came from the Prior's Lodgings. The
CHANCEL truncated at its eastern end by Bell, would initially have
comprised a choir and presbytery. Above the VESTRY DOOR in the
south wall are the remains of fine Early English arcading that would
have originally decorated much of the chancel.

The CHAPTER HOUSE was situated at the southern end of the east
range which also included the friars' DORMITORY, adjacent to the
church. The south range survives largely intact and once housed the
friars' much treasured LIBRARY, probably on the first floor where
there is a large room open to the roof and divided into study cubicles,
or carrels, lit by small south-facing windows that overlooked the kitchen
and service buildings. The west range, substantially altered in the early
nineteenth century to form three houses facing onto Ladybellegate
Street, originally housed the friars' refectory at its southern end.

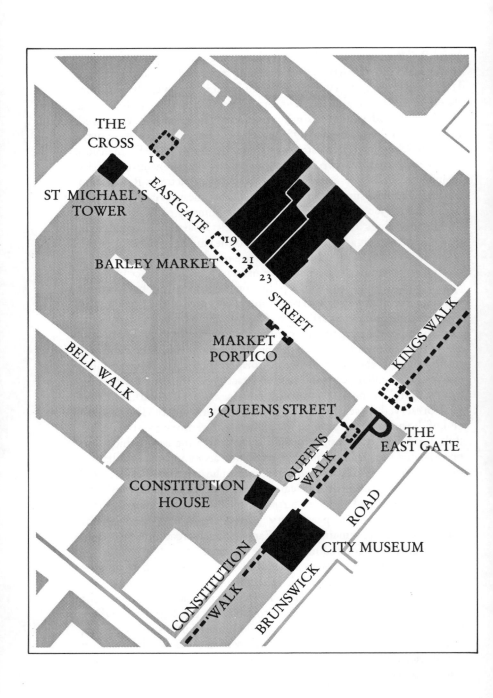

THE
CROSS

1

ST MICHAEL'S
TOWER

EASTGATE

19
21
23

BARLEY MARKET

STREET

MARKET
PORTICO

BELL WALK

KINGS WALK

3 QUEENS STREET

QUEENS WALK

P

THE
EAST GATE

CONSTITUTION
HOUSE

ROAD

CITY MUSEUM

CONSTITUTION WALK

BRUNSWICK

Eastgate Street

In the early medieval period this was probably the least important of the main trading streets in the town. A flourishing Jewish community was centred on the northern side of the street, near the Cross. Throughout the country there was a general distrust of the Jews and Gloucester had its own share of anti-semitic stories. For example, the *Historia* of St Peter's Abbey records that in 1168 the Jews of Gloucester were accused of torturing and murdering a young Christian boy and throwing his body into the River Severn. Despite this the community flourished until 1275 when they were banished to Bristol by Queen Eleanor. Edward 1 had cancelled all debts owed to the Jews and had persuaded his mother to remove them from the towns she held in dower. Although the community had gone the street continued to be referred to as Jeweriestrete well into the fourteenth century.

In the fifteenth century Eastgate Street contained a variety of trades and professions. These included a baker, a brewer, several glovers, a lawyer, and a weaver who lived next to a working mill on the south side of the street.

In 1655 a pillared market house for the sale of barley was erected in the middle of the roadway, half way between the Cross and the gate, replacing an older and less convenient structure that stood at the eastern end of the street. The area immediately to the west of the new market house was the site of a fruit and vegetable market that continued well into the eighteenth century.

The opening of the railway station to the east of the city centre, in the 1840s, turned Eastgate Street into a busy and commercially attractive thoroughfare which by the end of the century boasted some of the most prominent new buildings in Gloucester.

St Michael's Tower

The imposing fifteenth-century tower belonged to the church of St Michael the Archangel which was first recorded in the twelfth century. This early church consisted of a western tower and porch with a nave and chancel that stretched some eighty feet (24m.) to the east,

enclosing a burial ground on the south side. The north wall of the nave encroached some distance into the street and its outer face was completely hidden from view by a row of shops, booths and tenements that were built against it. These obstructions were cleared away in the eighteenth century in an attempt to relieve the congestion around the Cross area.

In 1849 the old church was taken down and replaced with a larger building sited a little further to the south to permit the widening of the street. This later church was closed in 1940 following the unification of the parish with that of St Mary de Crypt; the body of the church was cleared away in 1956.

The tower was built about 1465 and played an interesting part in the regulation of daily life in Gloucester. Because of the ever present danger of fire in a town largely built of timber, householders were permitted to use their hearths only between 4 a.m. and 8 p.m. each day. These times were signalled by the tolling of the curfew bell housed in the belfry of the tower. Apart from a short break in the nineteenth century the practice of ringing the evening bell continued here until the outbreak of the Second World War.

A clock and chimes had been installed within the tower by the middle of the sixteenth century for the benefit of the townspeople and by 1611 the bellchamber contained a peal of six bells. From 1752 the opening and closing times of the city markets were also controlled from the tower by a bell that was later used as a fire alarm.

The space below the tower is ceilinged with an elaborate liern vault. Below this is the richly coloured stained glass west window of 1878. The main Gloucester Tourist Information Centre was installed here in 1985 as part of an improved service to visitors; whilst the office may not be the largest in the country it may well qualify as the tallest!

W. E. Henley, writer and poet

William Ernest Henley was born on 23 August 1849 at No. 1
Eastgate Street. He was the eldest of the six children born to
William Henley, a stationer, printer and secondhand book
seller. At the age of twelve William junior entered the Crypt
School under the headmastership of the 'Manx Poet' T. E.
Brown, best known for 'A garden is a lovesome thing.' Henley's
schooldays were bedevilled by a tuberculosis germ that had
infected his left leg, which ultimately led to its amputation just
below the knee in December 1865. He left school in 1867 and set off for
London to pursue a career in freelance journalism, no doubt influenced
by his father's profession and the encouragement of his headmaster.

In 1872 the tuberculosis attacked his right foot and following
unsuccessful treatment at a Margate Infirmary he made his way to
Edinburgh to seek the help of the eminent surgeon Joseph Lister, who
eventually saved the limb. It was in Scotland that he met his future
wife Anna Boyle and formed a strong and lasting friendship with
Robert Louis Stevenson who freely admitted that he based Long John
Silver on the burly, wooden legged Henley. He returned to London
in 1876 to continue his literary work; writing several plays in collabo-
ration with Stevenson, a book of poetry plus many articles on art and
music. He became editor of several periodicals and published the
Barrack Room Ballads of Rudyard Kipling and *The Time Machine*
by H. G. Wells in the *National Observer*. He also serialised the work
of Joseph Conrad in his *The New Review*. These writers became part
of Henley's personal circle of literary friends that also included J. M.
Barrie, the author of *Peter Pan*. The name 'Wendy' was inspired by
Henley's little daughter Margaret, who on meeting Barrie would
attempt to call him 'my friendy' but could only utter 'fwendy' instead.

Margaret died of cerebral meningitis in 1894 when she was just five
years old and the bereaved Henley passed away on 11 July 1903
following a recurrence of tuberculosis caused by a fall from a train in
the previous year.

> It matters not how strait the gate,
> How charged with punishment the scroll,
> I am the master of my fate
> I am the captain of my soul.
> from 'Invictus' (1879)

19 Eastgate Street

A general economic improvement in the 1880s led to an
expansion of the banking industry in Gloucester. This tall
impressive Renaissance style brick and terracotta building
was erected for Lloyds Bank in 1898 to a design by Waller
and Son.

21 Eastgate Street

The National Westminster Bank is housed in a building originally
constructed for the National Provincial Bank. It was designed by the
London architect Charles Gribble and opened here around 1889. The
three-storey Cotswold stone façade is in the baroque classical style
with Ionic order columns on the two lower floors and a great cam-
bered pediment above. The building replaced an earlier branch that
stood at 22 Westgate Street on the site of the earliest bank in the city
opened in 1716 by James Wood, a city mercer.

23 Eastgate Street

The Guildhall was opened in 1892 to provide more spacious accommodation for the city's administrators who, previously, had operated
from the cramped eighteenth-century Tolsey on the south-western
corner of the Cross. The new building was designed by George Hunt
in the Renaissance style with a stone façade decorated at the attic level
with heraldry and carved cherubs. The ground floor housed the Town
Clerk and other officers, with the Mayor's Parlour, council chamber
and committee rooms plus a large public hall above. The building
continued in civic use until 1985 when the city council sold it to the

Cheltenham and Gloucester Building Society
and moved its administration offices to converted warehouses in the docks. After the reloca-
tion of the Society's main Gloucester branch into
the spacious ground floor area the upper levels
were converted into an Arts Centre.

Prior to the construction of the Guildhall the
site had been occupied by the Blue Coat School
that was founded in 1666 by Sir Thomas Rich, a
wealthy London merchant and native of the city.
The school continues under the name of its founder and is presently situated in the northern
suburbs of the city.

The Eastgate Market Portico

The portico was first built in 1856 on a site 40m. (130 ft.) to the west of its present position and was re-erected here in 1973 following the comprehensive redevelopment of the area between Eastgate Street and Bell Lane (now Bell Walk) into a new shopping precinct. The three tall arches supported by large Corinthian columns formed an impressive entrance to a rebuilt Eastgate Market which originally was one of two off-street sites created in 1786 in a bid to clear away the many produce stalls that obstructed the main thoroughfares in the city. The market rehoused the stalls of the country market-gardeners from their pitch in Eastgate Street as well as providing a point of sale for meat, pigs, poultry and corn. The other market opened at this time was on the west side of Southgate Street near the Cross which accommodated the dairy producers, fishmongers and earthenware sellers.

The East Gate

The first East Gate was constructed by the Roman army as one of the four access points into the fortress built at Gloucester in the late 60s AD. The rectangular shaped fortress was defended by a ditch in front of a turf and clay rampart capped with a wooden palisade, and by gateways flanked by massive timber towers. By the end of the first century this military base had evolved into a thriving civilian town of high status with the walls and gates rebuilt in stone on a grander scale. The later Roman gate survived into the Saxon period to form an important part of the town's defences. It was replaced by a simpler tunnel style gateway after the Norman Conquest in the eleventh century. The impressive 'D' shaped gatetowers were added in the thirteenth century together with a new drawbridge across the moat. This bridge was further strengthened by the addition of an outer defence or barbican in the fifteenth century.

By the sixteenth century the military importance of the gate had declined and, in consequence, the various rooms within were used for a variety of purposes. The north tower had been converted into a women's prison by 1584 that later became the city House of Correction. Council meetings were also held in another part of the building due to the

disrepair of the meeting chamber at the Tolsey. The ditch adjacent to the south tower was reconstructed to accommodate a stone-lined pool used for the washing of horses and carts prior to their entry into the city. The gate returned to military prominence during the siege of 1643 when Royalist miners tunnelled under the moat in an attempt to blow up the gatehouse, but were thwarted when their mines became flooded due to a high water table!

In 1703 the porter's lodge within the gatehouse was leased to the Guardians of the Poor who opened a poor school there together with a bridewell, or prison, in the dungeon. A hue and cry was instigated following the escape of two inmates of the prison who obtained their freedom by squeezing down through the latrine channel that led to the moat. They were soon recaptured by their pursuers who were aided, no doubt, by an easy-to-follow trail!

The above-ground structure was demolished in 1778 to enable the carriageway to be widened towards the north. The south tower, the horsepool and a section of Roman wall visible today were revealed during an archaeological excavation carried out in 1974. These extensive remains were subsequently preserved by the Boots Company who provided the underground viewing chamber officially opened to the public in 1980.

Ivor Gurney, poet and composer

Ivor Bertie Gurney, the son of a Gloucester tailor, was born at 3 Queen Street on 28 August 1890. His musical ability became apparent following admission to the choir of the family church of All Saints, where in 1900 under the guidance of the curate Alfred Cheeseman he successfully applied for a place as a chorister at the King's School attached to the cathedral. He studied music and composition under the organist Dr Herbert Brewer and later, on leaving the choir, became an articled pupil to him together with two other musical progenies, Herbert Howells and Ivor Novello.

Although Gurney began producing accomplished musical settings to the poetic works of Housman, Bridges and Henley at this time, his personal behaviour gave some cause for concern. He became more isolated from his family and spent much of his time wandering alone through the countryside, sometimes staying out all night, or visiting the home of his schoolfriend F. W. Harvey at Minsterworth.

In 1911 the talented Gurney entered the Royal College of Music where the originality of his compositions came to the fore despite an unpredictable and obstinate attitude towards his tutors. At the conclusion of intense sessions of hard work he became afflicted with bouts of severe depression that could be lifted only by regular visits to Gloucestershire and its ancient cathedral city. The joy he felt on these occasions was expressed through his keenly observed and unsentimental poetic works.

After the outbreak of the First World War he volunteered for active service as a signaller in the 2nd/5th Battalion of the Gloucestershire Regiment and was posted to the front in 1916. Despite the horrors of trench warfare he found solace in the comradeship he found in the regiment, and whenever possible he dedicated himself to music, composition and poetry. In 1917 he was wounded in the arm and later suffered the effects of a gas attack at Passchendaele that ultimately led to his repatriation to a hospital in Edinburgh. The poems written in France were published under the title *Severn and Somme* which received favourable reviews from the critics and Gurney was justifiably proud to be known as a War Poet. He recovered from his war injuries, but soon the fluctuating moods returned to be followed by a mild breakdown that was treated at Lord Derby's War Hospital at Warrington. By 1918 it was obvious to his friends that he had become a deeply disturbed individual.

He returned to the Royal College of Music, where, under the direction of the kindly Vaughan Williams he produced a prolific amount of musical works and poetry. However all was not well with the young composer – he spent less time at college and indulged the restless urge to wander, thinking nothing of walking from London to Gloucester and sleeping rough at night.

After leaving the college in 1921 he became incapable of regular employment and burdened himself upon various members of his family. He became afflicted by severe head pains and maintained that he was being harmed by electrical waves emanating from the wireless.

Following a suicide attempt he was eventually committed to the Barnwood House asylum on the outskirts of Gloucester in 1922. Ivor Gurney was later transferred to the City of London Hospital at Dartford, Kent, where he remained until his death from tuberculosis in December 1937. He is buried in the churchyard at Twigworth, near Gloucester.

> Who says 'Gloucester' sees a tall
> Fair fashioned shape of stone arise,
> That changes with the changing skies
> From joy to gloom funereal,
> Then quick again to joy; and sees
> Those four most ancient ways come in
> To mix their folk and dust and din
> With the keen scent of the sea-breeze.

Constitution House

The imposing three-storey house was built in 1750 for Richard Chandler, a Gloucester woolstapler. In order to supplement the extensive gardens to the south of the property, Chandler leased an area of waste ground immediately in front of the building where the City Museum now stands. The new sunken garden was set within the remnants of the city moat and access to the formal walkways and summerhouse was gained by way of a flight of stone steps leading down from Constitution Walk. In 1791 the grounds of Constitution House, by then occupied by Richard Chandler junior, were to witness an interesting event involving the eminent scientist and theologian, Dr Joseph Priestley.

Priestley had become well known not only for his experiments in

the field of electricity and water soluble gases but also for his radical political and religious views. In 1791 he gave great offence to many people throughout Britain by his outspoken support for the French Revolution. On 14 July of that year he was a guest of honour at a dinner given by the Birmingham Constitutional Society to commemorate the storming of the Bastille. The many inflammatory handbills that had been circulated in that city prior to the event caused a storm of protest that quickly degenerated into open riot. The rampaging mob burned down the houses of Priestley and several of his supporters, causing the scientist to flee to Gloucester where he sought refuge at the home of Richard Chandler.

Word of Priestley's arrival soon spread across the city and by nine o'clock in the evening a large crowd had arrived at the locked entrance to Constitution House. The excited and noisy mob repeatedly demanded that Priestley be turned out and were quietened only by the appearance of Richard Chandler at the front door. He quickly rebuked the many familiar faces before him and firmly assured them that Dr Priestley was not in his home and invited them to walk in and see for themselves. On hearing these words from such a respected and worthy man the crowd became subdued and immediately dispersed in a quiet and orderly manner. Indeed, Richard Chandler had not lied to his fellow citizens, for Joseph Priestley was hiding in the summerhouse.

The property remained in the hands of the Chandler family until 1876 and subsequent to its use as a school for young ladies it was sold to the Gloucester Conservative Club in 1883.

The City Museum And Art Gallery

The museum is housed in the William Edwin Price memorial hall, built by his widow Margaret in 1893 to accommodate the Gloucester Science and Art Society. The Gloucester Corporation took over the running of the building in 1896 and adapted it as a municipal museum in 1902.

It now contains an exceptionally interesting Archaeological Gallery built over an excavated length of the Roman town wall and exhibits finds from throughout the history of the city. The Natural History section displays the county's fascinating and varied flora and fauna from prehistoric times to the present day plus live exhibits of bees and freshwater fish. The first floor gallery contains an excellent series of period furniture together with collections of barometers, glass, ceramics and silver. The Art Gallery features the Museum's important permanent collection of pictures and hosts many special exhibitions throughout the year.

Westgate Street

For many centuries this was the busiest and most important highway in the city, for it gave access to the bridge across the River Severn that formed an important link in the main trading routes from London and Bristol to South Wales.

The line of the upper part of Westgate Street from the Cross to Berkeley Street derives from the Saxon period and it was probably influenced by an open market area of the Roman town. The main Roman west street and the remains of the buildings that fronted onto it now lie beneath the properties on the southern side of the modern street.

From the twelfth century onwards this wide thoroughfare was gradually divided into two separate streets by a line of infill buildings erected in the centre of the roadway, possibly at the behest of the crown or, more likely, by one of the Constables of Gloucester acting with the king's authority. Between the Cross and St John's Lane stood a block of tenements and shops together with the church of St Mary de Grace, referred to in the twelfth century as St Mary in the Market. This church functioned as an ammunition store during the civil war siege of 1643 and was demolished in 1655. West of St John's Lane stood a fourteenth-century structure known as the King's Board which may have been an official place of exchange or a collection point for tolls or taxes, for it was built on the site of the Gloucester mint which ceased to produce coinage in the thirteenth century. Immediately to the west stood another block of tenements and shops with the church of Holy Trinity beyond. Although the body of this church was demolished in 1699 many of the burgesses who were laid to rest within its walls still lie buried beneath the roadway today. The tower which stood opposite College Court was taken down in 1750 together with all the remaining buildings that stood in the centre of the street.

Upper Westgate Street had become the main market area of the town by the thirteenth century and many important trades had become established here by the Middle Ages. The northern side of the street between the Cross and St John's Lane was known as the Coiffery for it was here that the head-dress and hat makers had their shops and booths. The sellers of silk and other high quality cloths were sited in Mercers Row which occupied the area from St John's Lane to College Court. The southern side of the street consisted of various shops and the butchers' shambles where cattle were slaughtered and jointed in public. This practice led, inevitably, to the roadway being strewn with offal, blood and bones. An open space, called the Knapp, opposite St John's Lane, was the site of the herb and fish market where locally caught salmon and lamprey could be purchased together with the appropriate culinary flavourings. By the end of the sixteenth century the King's Board was used as a market house for the sale of cheese and butter. This was the forerunner of the Great Cheese Fairs of the eighteenth century where many tons of Single and Double Gloucester cheeses were sold for distribution to other parts of the country.

From the twelfth century the administration of the medieval town was carried out at the Booth Hall or Guildhall which stood further down Westgate Street near the junction with Upper Quay Street. This building was superseded in the sixteenth century by the Tolsey which was erected on the south-western corner of the Cross. In 1648 this property was further extended westwards into the ancient church of All Saints that originated, possibly, as a private chapel attached to the house of a wealthy merchant in Westgate Street.

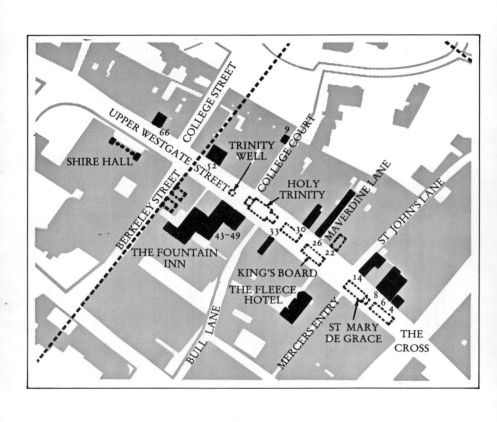

UPPER WESTGATE STREET
COLLEGE STREET
COLLEGE COURT
SHIRE HALL
66
52
TRINITY
WELL
9
HOLY
TRINITY
BERKELEY STREET
MAVERDINE LANE
ST JOHN'S LANE
43-49
33
30
26
22
THE FOUNTAIN
INN
KING'S BOARD
14
8
6
4
THE FLEECE
HOTEL
BULL LANE
MERCERS ENTRY
ST MARY
DE GRACE
THE
CROSS

Upper Westgate Street

4 Westgate Street

The large limestone block on display in the window of the modern extension to the bank was discovered during construction work for the basement area. The plinth was found supporting the shaft of a Roman column of 90 cm. diameter that survived to a height of two metres. Several other similar columns have been discovered in or below the cellars of other properties on the northern side of Westgate Street, suggesting the presence of a monumental Roman structure which may have formed part of the range of buildings that once faced onto the open market area which lies beneath the roadway.

6-8 Westgate Street

The prosaic nineteenth-century façade of this building gives little clue to the architectural delights to be found inside. The first floor of a sixteenth-century wing at the rear houses an elaborate timber-panelled room that was originally the guest chamber of Thomas Payne, Sheriff of Gloucester in 1534 and Mayor in 1540. The walls of the Tudor Room are mostly covered with oak linen-fold panels with a frieze of carved details at ceiling level depicting heraldic beasts, the arms of various local guild companies and the initials T.P. The room was refurbished in 1890 by J. Ambrose Fisher, a restaurateur, who commissioned a local carver, Mr G. Howitt, to repair or replace several of the damaged details and construct a suitable overmantel for the fireplace. Mr Howitt's structure consists of finely carved details depicting the badges of Henry VIII and Katherine of Aragon together with three central linen-fold panels framed by barley sugar style columns. It is recorded that he used 'old woodwork found in this part of the house' and the source of the columns can be found close by; the narrow staircase that leads from the room is seriously depleted of balusters!

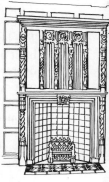

The room is now used as a business meeting facility and is not open to the public.

Mercers Entry

This narrow alleyway is one of the last remaining tenth-century side streets still in public use. Many others exist in the city but they have been converted into entrances or passageways to private properties. The alleyway received its current name in the nineteenth century following the re-erection of a medieval timber building known as the Mercers' Hall at its southern end. Prior to this it was named Fox's Passage after an alehouse of that name which stood half-way along on the eastern side; and in the medieval period it was popularly referred to as Love Alley due to the presence of disreputable beer shops that harboured those who were members of the oldest profession.

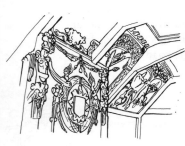

14 Westgate Street

The eighteenth-century brick façade conceals a house that was occupied by a wealthy merchant in the sixteenth century. The rear wing that stands parallel to St John's Lane contains on the first floor a three-bay room with a fine plaster ceiling that dates from 1600 and which can be seen from the lane when the premises are lit.

The Fleece Hotel

The hostelry was built about 1500 and was one of three 'Great Inns' built by the Abbey of St Peter in order to reduce the pressures on its overcrowded guesthouses. In 1534 the inn was held by Henry Marmyon, mayor in 1533 and 1541. Following the dissolution of the Abbey the property was conveyed to the dean and chapter of Gloucester Cathedral. By 1665 the inn was known as the 'Golden Fleece' which reflected the importance of the wool trade to the city, however the 'Golden' was later dropped due to a decline in the industry. In 1673 the landlord was a colourful local character called Gray Cox who seemingly had a lack of respect for authority. He was elected a member of the Common Council of the city by the mayor and burgesses but promptly declined the honour. It was customary for every newly elected member to pay a fine of twenty nobles (£6.60) to the civic purse and Cox's refusal was met with a larger fine of £50, which he also neglected to pay. The dispute carried on for a number of years and raised the ire of his landlords, the Cathedral Chapter, who censured him for his unworthy behaviour.

By 1770 the inn had fallen out of repair and after remaining empty for a few years the dean and chapter offered the building to the mayor and burgesses for the sum of £150 in order to make a market and shambles on the site. Following the Common Council's rejection of this offer the dean, Josiah Tucker, expressed a personal interest in leasing and running the building. It was considered inappropriate that he should rent the inn from himself so the lease was finally made out in the name of a minor canon. The property was sold by the church in 1799 and since then has been privately owned and remains one of the few 'free' houses in the city.

Beneath the eastern range of buildings lies an interesting twelfth-century tunnel-vaulted undercroft with arches supported on round Norman pillars. This initially would have been used as a fireproof storage area by a merchant but in more recent years it has served as one of the most unusual bars in Gloucester.

James Wood, banker, draper and eccentric.

The Gloucester Old Bank, one of the earliest private banks in England, was founded in 1716 by James Wood's grandfather who traded from a medieval timber building that stood on the site of 22 Westgate Street. James Wood was born on 7 October 1756 and became proprietor of the banking and drapery business in 1802 after the death of his father, Richard. Jemmy, as he was known in his native city, became a familiar sight to passers-by as he stood at the doorway of his premises. His face had a well developed nose and a sharply receding forehead which gave him a Punch-like profile. He wore shabby breeches and hose with a waistcoat that stretched up and across his ample stomach revealing an expanse of shirt below.

The banking office, set into one corner of his haberdashery shop, was attended by two clerks who processed transactions across a wooden counter onto which had been nailed an assortment of counterfeit coins. It was at this counter that Jemmy Wood prospered by shrewd lending, astute investment and by strict attention to petty detail.

He remained a bachelor and following the deaths of his sisters acknowledged no relations. Despite his growing wealth his name seldom appeared on the various lists of local charitable donations. He shunned the use of public transport wherever possible preferring to visit his various farms and friends in the county on foot. Sometimes he was able to hitch a ride aboard a passing cart and on one occasion during a particularly heavy rainstorm returned to Gloucester inside an empty funeral hearse.

For all his miserly ways Jemmy did not stint himself when it came to food, for his diaries relate a number of sumptuous feasts consumed in the line of civic duty. He became a member of the Gloucester City Corporation in 1803, served as sheriff in 1811 and 1813, and was elected an alderman in 1820. He was never mayor of Gloucester, probably because of the expense involved in holding the office.

Jemmy Wood became well known throughout Great Britain for his meanness and eccentricity. His portly figure was commemorated in the form of pottery statuettes and his striking face appeared on many Toby jugs. He was also the subject of irreverent cartoons that lampooned his banking prowess; one depicted him counting gold coin with his new partner – the devil.

Jemmy Wood died on 20 April 1836 and was buried in St Mary de Crypt church in Southgate Street. He left an estate valued at £900,000 which caused great speculation in the city as to whom would benefit from his will. A dispute arose following the production of a partly burnt codicil which contained several legacies including one of £140,000 to the Gloucester City Corporation who promptly embarked upon an expensive legal action to obtain their share. Although the codicil was upheld, the Corporation was denied the money as they were trustees to the estate. As a result of the lengthy legal wranglings much of the miser's fortune was consumed by litigation.

The Gloucester Old Bank was absorbed by the County of Gloucester Banking Company in 1838, which in turn was taken over by Lloyds Bank in 1897.

Maverdine Lane

This narrow alleyway led from Westgate Street to the wall of St Peter's Abbey and was once a right-of-way for Bailiffs to inspect the abbey water supply which ran down from nearby St John's Lane.

26 Westgate Street

The early nineteenth-century façade hides what is probably Gloucester's finest timber-framed building. It is a sixteenth-century four-storey house with oriel windows and leaded lights, some with original glass, that face onto Maverdine Lane. Among the early occupants of the house were Alderman John Brown and his wife, Sarah, and a local perfumier called George Meadows. By the eighteenth century it had become the Hall of the Grocers Guild and was later the mansion house of Richard Webb, Mayor of the city in 1760, 1767 and 1782.

In the early nineteenth century the house was used as a lodging for Assize Judges but, seemingly, it was not in the best of repair. One judge flatly refused to stay in the building and referred to it as a 'badly drained, ill-ventilated, foetid dog-hole.' Furthermore, he announced his attention of staying outside the city which would necessitate starting the Assize one hour late and finishing one hour early each day to allow time for travelling. The building became known as the Gloucestershire Seed Warehouse in 1886 due to its occupation by the well-known seeds merchants Winfield & Sons who traded here until 1989.

33 Westgate Street

The narrow eighteenth-century brick front conceals a rare example of a small, late fourteenth-century merchant's town house. Behind the shop front, at ceiling level, is a moulded beam that once supported part of the timber-framed façade, and below the pavement level part of the original entrance doorway to a stone-vaulted under-croft still survives.

30 Westgate Street

This house in Mercer's Row was first occupied in 1622 by John Whithorne, tailor, who leased it together with the stables and gardens at the rear from the Corporation. By 1640 the premises were taken by

James Commeline, apothecary, who fled to England in order to escape the religious tur-moil of the Netherlands. His new-found peace was promptly shattered in 1643 when he found himself in the front line of the English Civil War during the Siege of Gloucester. On Friday evening, 25 August, a besieging Royalist bat-tery at Llanthony fired red-hot cannonballs into the city, one of which, according to a contemporary account '. . . came through three houses and fell into the chamber of Mr Commeline, the apothecary, and being per-ceived, many payles of water were cast upon it to quench the same . . .' James Commeline served as Sheriff for the city in 1654 and the house remained in the hands of his descendants until 1746 when it was leased to George Worrall who was a partner in a thriving pin-making business.

In 1799 it became the Theatre Vaults public house which provided an access, via a narrow passageway, to the Pit entrance to the Theatre Royal. The shell of the theatre, together with the doorway, still survives at the rear of the building. The old theatre boasts an impres-sive list of illustrious names among the performers of the past. Sir Henry Irving gave his masterly rendition of 'The Bells'; Ellen Terry acted here and Charles Dickens packed the house for his rendering of excerpts from his own novels.

Bull Lane

The lane takes its current name from the Bull Inn that stood opposite the entrance to Cross Keys Lane from about 1700. The earlier name of Gore Lane was used from the thirteenth century and evolved from the presence of pig-sties and slaughter houses.

43-45 Westgate Street

Originally two separate properties built in the sixteenth century with gable ends facing onto the street. The left-hand building retains much of its original appearance but the right-hand building was re-fronted in the early eighteenth century. A close inspection will reveal that the left- and right-hand windows at top storey level are purely imitation and there is nothing behind them except fresh air!

These two buildings were linked together in 1990 by the Whitbread Brewery who renamed the existing Union Inn (No. 43) as 'The Tailor's House' to commemorate the Beatrix Potter story. The real 'Tailor of Gloucester', John Pritchard, once occupied No. 45.

Beatrix Potter often stayed with a cousin at Hares-combe Grange, near Gloucester, and it was on one of these visits in the 1890s that she heard the story concerning the mysterious completion of a waistcoat that was to inspire her classic children's tale. The tailor had left the garment unfinished when he locked up his shop for the weekend but found it nearly completed when he returned on the Monday morning. One buttonhole remained unsewn, and pinned alongside it was a little note saying 'no more twist.' Prichard shrewdly drew attention to the mystery by placing the waistcoat in the shop window with a notice that read 'Come to Pritchard the tailor where the waistcoats are made at night by the fairies.'

The true story was revealed many years later by the tailor's son, Douglas. It transpired that two or three of the tailor's workmen got drunk on the Saturday night and were unable to get home. Unbeknown to their employer one of them had a key to the shop so they decided to sleep off their excesses in the workroom. Waking on the Sunday morning, unshaven and in their working clothes, they did not dare to leave the shop for fear of being seen by the local churchgoers. They were thus trapped until darkness fell and to pass away the intervening hours they finished the waistcoat, but ran out of thread before the final buttonhole could be completed.

College Court

A medieval lane leading to the layfolks' cemetery within the precincts of St Peter's Abbey. Several of the medieval churches in the centre of the medieval town did not possess their own burial grounds so an area was set aside here for the purpose.

9 College Court: the House of the Tailor of Gloucester

The small shop at the end of College Court next to St Michael's Gate is the home that Beatrix Potter chose for her *Tailor of Gloucester*. This and other houses in the city were sketched in 1897 as the basis for the illustrations for her book. The shop and museum, devoted to the World of Beatrix Potter, was opened in 1979 by Frederick Warne & Co. Inside, the tailor's kitchen has been faithfully recreated from her drawings together with a replica of the famous waistcoat.

47-49 Westgate Street

A large early eighteenth-century town house that was converted into two shops and dwellings about 1750. Below the street front of both shops lies a large medieval cellar that was divided by brick walls and barrel vaults in the eighteenth century. Extending southwards from the rear of this cellar, and mostly under No. 47, is a large thirteenth-century barrel-vaulted undercroft. It stands 2.5 m. (8 ft.) at the apex of the vault and its 10.5 m. (33 ft.) length is divided into eight bays by dressed stone transverse ribs. This hidden gem had been sealed off for many years prior to its rediscovery in 1991 during an archaeological survey of the buildings in the south-west quadrant of the city.

The Fountain Inn

The Fountain Inn occupies one of the oldest known sites connected with the brewing trade in Gloucester.

During the reign of Henry III the property consisted of various booths and cellars in the tenure of Peter Poictevin, who, it is said, was Peter de Roches, the Bishop of Winchester, and who originally came from Poitou in France. Henry III is the only English king to have been crowned other than at Westminster Abbey since the Norman Conquest. His coronation

took place in St Peter's Abbey, Gloucester in 1216 under the auspices of Peter de Roches. It was not unusual for medieval kings to give grants of land in provincial towns to favourites who had rendered them a particular service.

In the first quarter of the fourteenth century part of the site was in the hands of John Taverner who ran a hostelry from a range of buildings that stood at the southern end of the entranceway. The earliest recorded name for the property appears in the middle of the fifteenth century during the ownership of Sybilla Savage who appropriately called it Savages Inn. In Tudor times the inn was known as The Catherine Wheel which, in 1538, was in the tenure of Thomas, the son of Sir Thomas Bell, a prominent local businessman and benefactor.

The premises became The Fountain in the seventeenth century and the name is generally accepted as being derived from a public water supply known as Trinity Well or Fountain that stood nearby in the centre of Westgate Street. In 1672 part of the inn was refurbished and upgraded to a fashionable coffee house and tavern at a cost of £200.

The relief portrait of King William III set above the doorway at the southern end of the courtyard is said, according to local legend, to commemorate a brief visit made by the monarch to Gloucester. During the early reign of William and Mary there were still a number of adherents to James II and the Stuart cause. One of these Jacobite cells met in an upper room at the Fountain Inn and it is said that William showed his contempt for his predecessor's cause by riding his horse up a flight of external stairs leading to the meeting place.

Throughout the following centuries the Fountain continued to serve the needs of the drinking public, who in the 1720s were entreated to patronise the 'well accustomed Tavern'. The inn has the distinction of being the last of the old city pubs to actually brew beer on the premises before succumbing to the attention of a major brewery.

Sir Charles Wheatstone

The great Victorian physicist was born above the family shop at 52/54 Westgate Street in February 1802 and baptised at nearby St Mary de Lode church. At the age of fourteen he was apprenticed to his uncle who was a manufacturer of musical instruments in The Strand, London. Young Charles became interested in the process by which the sound created by the vibrating strings of an instrument was transmitted to the sound board. In 1823 he produced a gadget called the 'Telephone' which was more popularly known in the music-halls as the 'Magic Harp'. It consisted of a harp standing alone on a stage but, hidden from view, it was connected by means of pliable wooden rods to a piano beneath. When the pianist played, the vibrations from the piano's strings were transferred to the instrument above and it appeared as if the harp was playing itself.

In 1829 he invented a brand-new musical instrument – the concertina, and later constructed a speaking machine that clearly pronounced a limited range of words. His interest lay not only in the field of sound; in 1834 he used a revolving mirror to measure the speed of electricity in a conductor. The same mirror was later used in measurements of the speed of light and from this he invented the Polar clock. He also created the stereoscope for viewing photographs in three dimensions; this Victorian drawing-room novelty proved invaluable to airborne reconnaissance during World War II.

Three years after gaining a Professorship of Experimental Physics at Kings College, London, he filed the first patent for a magnetic telegraph in 1837. In the same year, in association with William Fothergill Cooke, he developed the first public telegraph line between Euston Station, London and Chalk Farm using an instrument called the 'Needle Telegraph'.

In 1865 the young Alexander Graham Bell was introduced to him in London where Wheatstone demonstrated his 'Magic Harp'. This in turn gave Bell the idea for what he called 'Harmonic Multiple Telegraphy' and it was following an experiment with the new 'Harmonic Telegraph', when two contact springs became welded together during a heat wave, that Bell first produced an undulating current that would transmit the sound of the human voice.

The Gloucester Freeman's son from Westgate Street was knighted by Queen Victoria for his pioneering work on the first transatlantic telegraph cable. Sir Charles Wheatstone died in Paris on 9 October 1875, but his name lives on through a device still in common use throughout the world for accurately measuring electrical resistance, 'The Wheatstone Bridge'.

Berkeley Street

By 1301 this thoroughfare was referred to as Broadsmith Street probably because it formed part of the iron working area centred on nearby Longsmith Street. By the end of the seventeenth century it had been named Catherine Wheel Lane after the inn, and acquired today's title in the late eighteenth century.

College Street

The street attained its present width in 1893 in a move to improve vehicular access to the cathedral. It necessitated the removal of buildings on the eastern side of a 3 m. (10 ft.) wide medieval lane that led to the abbey's burial ground. In the thirteenth century it was known as Lich Lane but in the sixteenth century it was renamed Saint or King Edward's Lane as it led to the burial place of King Edward II. From 1714 it was variously known as College or Lower College Lane.

66 Westgate Street

This building was originally constructed as two separate dwellings and shops during the fifteenth century. The mid-Victorian ground floor shop windows are an early example of large plate-glass made possible by the technology gained in building the Crystal Palace, London for the Great Exhibition in 1851. The timber panelling on the wall to the right of the doorway is made from the original shutters used to protect the glass when the shop was closed. The building was restored by Gloucester City Council as a contribution to European Architectural Heritage Year in 1975.

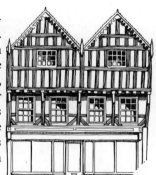

Shire Hall

The central Ionic portico formed part of the original Shire Hall building designed by the architect, Robert Smirke, in 1816. The grand entrance is said to be styled on the temple that stands on the River Illissus in Greece. Prior to the opening of the new building the county administration had been conducted since the sixteenth century from the Booth Hall, a large medieval complex of buildings that stood immediately to the west.

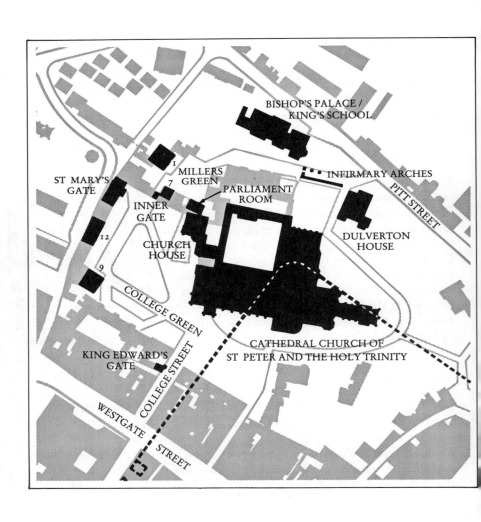

BISHOP'S PALACE /
KING'S SCHOOL

INFIRMARY ARCHES

PITT STREET

ST MARY'S
GATE

1

MILLERS
GREEN

7

PARLIAMENT
ROOM

INNER
GATE

DULVERTON
HOUSE

12

CHURCH
HOUSE

9

COLLEGE GREEN

KING EDWARD'S
GATE

COLLEGE STREET

CATHEDRAL CHURCH OF
ST PETER AND THE HOLY TRINITY

WESTGATE
STREET

The Cathedral and Precincts

The Cathedral Close

The close occupies twelve acres of historic Gloucester that were enclosed by stone walls in the thirteenth century to create the precincts of St Peter's Abbey. On the northern side, the boundary walls also formed part of the city defences. Although many fine buildings were erected in the close after the dissolution of the abbey, the area has remained largely unaltered for the last two hundred years.

King Edward's Gate

This building once formed part of the western tower of the lych gate that spanned the narrow medieval lane leading from Westgate Street to the burial ground within the abbey precincts. The gateway was built in the thirteenth century through the generosity of King Edward I and it was here that Abbot Thokey received the body of the murdered King Edward II in 1327 for interment in the abbey church. The structure was remodelled in the sixteenth century under the auspices of Abbot Parker who also added the stair turret on the northern side. The room above the gate arch was taken down in 1806, followed by the eastern tower in 1892. The stone shield, said to display the arms of the abbey's founder King Osric, was affixed to the south face of the tower after its discovery in the Cathedral Close in 1828.

Church House

The thirteenth-century gabled front conceals the Norman abbot's lodgings where the king and nobility were accommodated and entertained when visiting the abbey. The building to the west of the stair turret was formerly the abbot's meeting hall which today is divided

into two large rooms. At the southern end is the Laud Room lined with fine Jacobean panelling and at the northern end is the Henry Room that has a painted and decorated ceiling structure. The building was assigned to the prior in the fourteenth century following the construction of a new dwelling for the abbot on the north side of the precincts. Remnants of this later lodging can be seen in the perimeter wall of the abbey overlooking Pitt Street.

It was here that Henry VIII and Anne Boleyn stayed following their arrival at Gloucester on Saturday 31 July 1535. On the following Monday the royal party spent a long day in the saddle, hunting in the Painswick area. Darkness fell before the king and queen returned to the east gate of the city where they were met by fifteen citizens carrying blazing torches to light the way back to the abbey. The escorts were warmly thanked and received a gift of four gold angelleth nobles from the queen. The next day the royal party set out on another prolonged hunting trip, this time to Miserden. It was well into the night before they returned to Gloucester where word had spread of the previous day's royal generosity; this time the king was greeted at the gate by no fewer than forty blazing torches, each one held aloft by an eager burgess dressed in his best apparel.

9 College Green

This, one of the most impressive houses in the Cathedral Close, was built about 1707 by Samuel Ricketts on a site formerly occupied by two stables and the abbey miskin or dunghill. By 1753 the house was occupied by an eccentric widow Mrs Francis Cotton who kept a small aviary containing a robin in her pew near the high altar of the cathedral. Mrs Cotton maintained that the little bird was the reincarnation of her favourite daughter who had died some years earlier. Sir Horace Walpole commented 'The chapter indulge this whim as she contributes abundantly to glaze, whitewash and ornament the church.'

In the 1770s the house was let to Dr John Wall whose father was the founder of the Worcester china factory. Wall, too, was regarded as somewhat eccentric, but the diarist and novelist Fanny Burney recorded that she enjoyed the company of the 'droll character'. She stayed as a guest at the house in 1777 when she met several local worthies and witnessed a parade of the militia on the College Green.

12 College Green

In 1737 Alderman Benjamin Saunders, wine merchant and owner of the King's Head Inn in Westgate Street, established his 'Great Room' here for the holding of dances and assemblies. The building also served as a coffee house and as a venue for music recitals and public breakfasts where guests could play battledore and shuttlecock to the accompaniment of a band playing appropriate music.

St Mary's Gate

The wide, low-pointed arch of the thirteenth-century great gate provided the main entrance into the medieval abbey precincts. The windows set into the arcading of the western elevation provided a vantage point from which the dean and chapter and other officials witnessed the burning of Bishop Hooper in 1555. At the time the room was the office of the chapter clerk of the cathedral but it later became private accommodation. When James Sayer took over the lease in 1681 it contained a clause allowing him to set up sheep pens against the abbey wall in Three Cocks Lane on market and fair days. To the south of the gateway is a sixteenth-century timber-framed building constructed on the walls of a thirteenth-century undercroft. This building is held to be the lodging house of the abbey almoner. Through the leaded window adjacent to the gate arch can be seen the remains of an opening, now greatly enlarged, from where alms of food were distributed to the poor.

Inner Gate and Millers Green

The thirteenth-century gateway gives access to the inner court of the abbey which is today known as Millers Green. It is so called from the abbey water mill that stood on a tributary of the River Twyver near the site of number 2, Millers Green.

1 Millers Green, The Deanery

This fine house built about 1740 is complemented by the later pedimented stone doorway and the forecourt gate piers with handsome urns and wrought-iron railings. The house became the dean's residence in 1940. Previously he resided at Church House at the northwest corner of the cathedral.

7 Millers Green

Since the mid-nineteenth century this late seventeenth-century building has been the home of the cathedral organist. Probably the best known organist to live here was Samuel Sebastian Wesley, the great grandson of Charles Wesley. S. S. Wesley, born in 1819, was the son of Samuel who was the greatest organist of his day and staunch devotee of Johan Sebastian Bach. In 1832 at the age of twenty-two the young Samuel was appointed to Hereford Cathedral where, in his capacity as organist, he was the principal conductor at the Music Meeting, (later to be called the Three Choirs Festival), of 1834. Upon his marriage to the dean of Hereford's daughter he moved to Exeter, from where he moved to Leeds, to Winchester and finally to Gloucester. This series of appointments are best summed up in his own words, 'I have moved from cathedral to cathedral because I found music troubles at each.'

Since his early days in London, Wesley had always been passionately fond of fishing, indeed it was his devotion to this pastime that led to his resignation from Winchester. Upon being asked by the dean and chapter of Gloucester Cathedral to recommend someone for the vacant organist's post he replied that he would accept the position himself. His decision was influenced, no doubt, by the excellent fishing in the area.

He became organist at Gloucester in 1865 until his death in 1876 during which time he was the principal conductor at the Music Meeting on four occasions. His own compositions were many and include 'Aurelia', 'The Church's one foundation', 'Harewood', 'Christ is our corner stone' and anthems such as 'The Wilderness' and 'Blessed be the God and Father.'

Wesley was invited by the dean's wife, Mrs Ellicot, to accompany and conduct the College Ladies' Society Choir. The very first rehearsal proved too much for the temperamental organist. After a few bars had been sung by the ladies Wesley threw his arms in the air and shouted 'Cats' and promptly left the room.

The Parliament Room

A fifteenth-century timber-framed upper storey built onto a thirteenth-century stone undercroft that formed part of the building where Richard II held parliament in 1378.

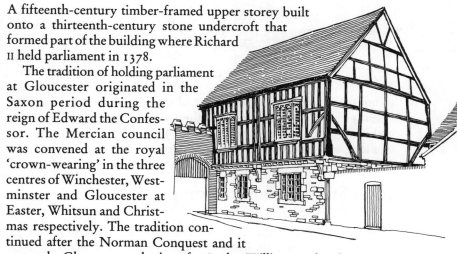

The tradition of holding parliament at Gloucester originated in the Saxon period during the reign of Edward the Confessor. The Mercian council was convened at the royal 'crown-wearing' in the three centres of Winchester, Westminster and Gloucester at Easter, Whitsun and Christmas respectively. The tradition continued after the Norman Conquest and it was at the Gloucester gathering of 1085 that William I ordered the detailed survey of the country that became known as the Domesday Book.

Bishop's Palace, The King's School

On the north side of Millers Green stands the grand Bishop's Palace of 1861 that was erected on the site of an earlier residence incorporated in the fourteenth-century abbot's lodging. Since the creation of a new residence for the Bishop of Gloucester at the eastern end of Pitt Street in the 1950s its Victorian predecessor has housed part of King's School created by King Henry VIII.

Infirmary Arches

The standing remains are part of the thirteenth-century south arcade and west wall of the monastic infirmary. At the eastern end is Dulverton House which originally functioned as the infirmarer's lodgings. The infirmary catered not only for the brethren of the abbey but also provided a home in which to care for wealthy elderly people from the secular community. Following the dissolution of the abbey this church-like building was sub-divided and extended to provide accommodation in which to house the families of the canons and servants of the cathedral. The ensuing chronic overcrowding of the area soon earned for itself the nickname of 'Babylon'. It was here that John Stafford Smith, the son of a long serving cathedral organist, Martin Smith, was born in 1750.

John Stafford Smith, composer

John Stafford Smith was christened in Gloucester Cathedral on 30 March 1750. He was educated at the cathedral school where he became an accomplished boy-singer. He was later accepted as a choir boy at the Chapel Royal, London and also studied under the famous Dr Boyce. By the 1770s he had gained a reputation as an excellent composer and organist. This led to his election as a member of the very select Anachreontic Society which boasted amongst its membership such august persons as Dr Johnson, James Boswell, Sir Joshua Reynolds, Henry Purcell and J. S. Bach.

About 1780 Smith composed the music for the society's constitutional song entitled 'To Anachreon in Heaven' that was inspired by the sixth-century BC Greek lyric poet who wrote odes on the pleasures of love and wine.

J. S. Smith was successively a gentleman of the Chapel Royal, lay-vicar of Westminster Abbey and one of the organists at the Chapel

Royal. He also acted as organist at the Three Choirs Festival held at Gloucester in 1790. He died in 1836 at the age of eighty-five, allegedly from the lodging of a grape-pip in his windpipe.

The song 'To Anachreon in Heaven' became very popular on both sides of the Atlantic following the establishment of several Anachreontic Societies in America.

During the second year of the war of 1812 the British fleet made a strategic night attack on Fort McHenry which protected the city of Baltimore on the eastern seaboard of the United States. A local attorney, Francis Scott Key, had gone aboard a British warship in an endeavour to secure the release of an American prisoner. Key was held on board ship so that he could not pass on any prior information to the patriots ashore. Throughout the night he remained on deck watching the bombardment in which congreve rockets were used in an attempt to batter the fort into submission. As dawn broke he saw, to his great surprise and delight, the huge American stars and stripes flag still flying over the badly damaged fort. He immediately penned a four verse poem to the tune composed by John Stafford Smith. It began,

Oh! say, can you see, by the dawn's early light,
What so proudly we hailed at the twilight's last gleaming?
Whose broad stripes and bright stars, thro' the perilous fight
O'er the ramparts we watched were so gallantly streaming?
And the rockets' red glare, the bombs bursting in air,
Gave proof thro' the night that our flag was still there.
Oh! say, does that star-spangled banner yet wave
O'er the land of the free and the home of the brave?

The poem was printed on handbills the next morning and distributed throughout Baltimore. The song became immediately popular and three months later it was played during the Battle of New Orleans. Although the American Army and Navy had long recognised 'The Star Spangled Banner' as the national anthem of the USA it was not until March 1931 that Congress officially adopted it as such.

Gloucester Cathedral

In 679 King Ethelred of Mercia granted lands in Gloucestershire to Osric, a sub-king of the Hwicce, to support the building of a church at Gloucester. Osric founded the Abbey of St Peter as a community of monks and nuns living separately but worshipping together under the rule of the abbess, his sister Kyneberga. Osric died in 729 and was buried in the abbey he had founded. The building eventually fell into decay and in 823 was rebuilt by Beornwulf, King of Mercia, as a house for secular priests. It lasted in this form until 1022 when Cnut expelled the priests and replaced them with somewhat undisciplined and unpopular Benedictine monks. After a disastrous fire in 1058 the abbey was rebuilt by Aldred, Bishop of Worcester, who ultimately neglected it and annexed much of its property when he later became Archbishop of York.

After the Norman Conquest, William the Conqueror took a step that was to influence strongly the religious life at Gloucester. In 1072 he appointed Serlo, a Benedictine monk from Mont St Michel in Normandy, to be abbot. At this time there were only two monks and eight novices at St Peter's Abbey. Serlo revitalised the near defunct house by regaining much of its lost estates and greatly increasing the number of monks. In the reign of William Rufus he began rebuilding the abbey in the Norman style. The foundation stone of the new church was laid in 1089 and it was finally consecrated in 1100, although building work continued at its western end until about 1120.

The Abbey of St Peter remained in the hands of the Benedictines until it was dissolved in 1540. In 1541 the church was rededicated to the Holy and Indivisible Trinity and became the centre of the new diocese of Gloucester.

The outstanding feature of the NAVE is the Norman arcading with its massive cylindrical columns, 2.13 m. (7 ft.) in diameter and 9.75 m. (32 ft.) high, which support round arches with chevron mouldings. The discolouration on the lower part of the pillars is a legacy of a series of disastrous fires that swept through the Norman church between 1122 and 1222. The stone-ribbed vault of the nave was built in 1242 together with a new ROOF above which was constructed from 110 oak trees from the Royal Forest of Dean given to the abbey by Henry III. The last two bays at the western end of the nave were rebuilt in the Perpendicular style in 1420 when the two original western towers became unsafe.

The glass in the west window was inserted in 1859 and depicts events in the early life of Christ and scenes from the Old Testament. Below the window on the south side of the nave stands the monument to Dr Edward Jenner, (1749-1823), who pioneered the technique of vaccination against smallpox.

The most striking feature of the SOUTH AISLE is the outward lean of the south wall which at one point is 28 cms. (11 in.) out of true. The third pillar of the Norman arcade also leans markedly southwards due to the presence of the soft fills of the defensive ditch of the Roman town below its foundations. The windows in the south wall were inserted in the early fourteenth century and each one is decorated with 1500 delicately carved ballflowers. The nineteenth-century stained glass in their windows illustrates, among other things, the coronation of the nine-year-old Henry III at the abbey in 1216, and the murder of Edward II at Berkeley Castle in 1327 together with the subsequent building of his tomb in the north ambulatory of the abbey church. At the western end of the south aisle is an interesting seventeenth-century monument to Alderman John Jones MP, who personally supervised its installation and decoration some forty-eight hours before his death in 1630.

The SOUTH TRANSEPT contains one of the earliest examples of Perpendicular architecture which appeared here in 1331 during the reconstruction of its Norman south wall and window. On the eastern side of the transept is the CHAPEL OF ST ANDREW restored in 1868 with wall paintings depicting the life of the saint. To the left of the chapel entrance is the little fifteenth-century 'Prentice Bracket' constructed in the shape of a mason's square. It once supported a row of figures on the top. On the underside of the bracket is the form of a young man apparently falling, perhaps referring to an accident at the abbey, with the figure of a mason below. On the north side of the transept is the early sixteenth-century CHAPEL OF ST JOHN THE BAPTIST enclosed by an oak screen decorated and coloured in the medieval style.

The floor plan of the CRYPT with its five radiating chapels reflects the plan of the original Norman church overhead. The arches and pillars in the southern ambulatory were strengthened following distortion caused by the weight of the choir building above. For many

years the crypt was used as a charnel house, an inscription above the entrance to the south chapel records the clearance of piles of bones and skulls from the central chamber in 1851. The north-west chapel may have been used as a mortuary chamber to hold the body of a member of the abbey community prior to burial in the nearby monks' cemetery.

The construction of the magnificent TOWER began in 1450 and continued for about ten years. This delicately detailed structure stands 68.5 m. (225 ft.) high to the top of the pinnacles and its estimated weight of 5,080,250 kg. (5000 tons) is supported by no fewer than ten massive flying buttresses both inside and outside of the church. This tower replaced an earlier and smaller structure which by the thirteenth century carried a tall slender spire.

At the ringing-chamber level is housed England's sole surviving medieval Bourdon bell, 'Great Peter', which weighs nearly 3048kg. (3 tons) and has a diameter of 174 cm. (68½ in.). Today the bell is swung by means of an electric motor but in the nineteenth century the operation was performed by no fewer than eight men at the end of a very long rope! The main bell-chamber contains a ring of bells that was increased in number from ten to twelve during a major refurbishment of bells and their hangings in 1979.

The original Norman PRESBYTERY and CHOIR were altered and enlarged in the first half of the fourteenth century following the taking down of the eastern apsidal end and the removal of the roof. The columns of the Norman arcades were cut back on the choir side and a layer of Perpendicular tracery was added to the walls. The vault of the new choir was raised to a height of 28.5 m. (92 ft.) thus making it the highest medieval stone vault in England. The roof bosses at the eastern end are decorated with fifteen angels each one playing a different musical instrument.

The EAST WINDOW is the largest in England measuring 28.8 m. (78 ft.) by 11.6 m. (38 ft.). It was erected in 1349 as a war memorial commemorating the participation of local knights and barons at the Battle of Crécy in 1346 and the Siege of Calais in 1347.

The highly decorated REREDOS of the high altar dates from 1873. The figure work is by Frank Redfern who was also responsible for the statuary on the façade of the south porch.

The canopied and intricately carved, WOODEN CHOIRSTALLS date from 1350 and contain fifty-eight misericord seats decorated with scenes that reflect the interests of their creators.

The great organ, completed in 1666, was removed to here in the eighteenth century from its original position under the south crossing arch. The wooden case was constructed by the cathedral carpenters with the gilding and painting applied by a local painter.

The SOUTH AMBULATORY houses the effigy of Robert, Duke of Normandy, eldest son of William the Conqueror. It commemorates his burial in the abbey following his death at Cardiff Castle in 1134. The thirteenth-century effigy, fashioned from Irish bog oak, rests on a fifteenth-century mortuary box decorated with heraldry. The figure was restored and repainted in the seventeenth century after it had been hacked to pieces by Parliamentarian soldiers and fortunately rescued by Sir Humphrey Tracy.

The LADY CHAPEL was completed at the very end of the fifteenth century and represents the final flowering of the Perpendicular style of architecture. The vaulted roof, almost identical to that of the choir, is supported by arcades of pointed arches which are almost entirely filled with glazing. The east window contains a colourful jumble of glass that was reset following extensive damage caused either at the Dissolution or during the Commonwealth in the seventeenth century. The communion rails were removed here from the choir in the 1870s by Gilbert Scott. They were originally installed in the early seventeenth century at the behest of Dean William Laud who, it is said, ordered that the space between the vertical rails should be sufficiently narrow in order to prevent stray dogs from entering the sanctuary.

The WESTERN CHAPEL above the entrance to the lady chapel was designed to accommodate a responsary choir and the two CHANTRY CHAPELS each have a singing gallery above its fan-vaulting. In the south chapel is a memorial to Thomas Fitzwilliams bearing an interesting inscription referring to the Siege of Gloucester in 1643. Among other memorials in the lady chapel is one to John Powell, an eminent member of the Queen's Bench and Chancellor of the Diocese who died in 1713.

The NORTH AMBULATORY contains the memorial chapel of the Gloucestershire Regiment containing the Books of Remembrance, the pages of which are turned daily. Nearby is the small stone Celtic cross that was carved with a nail by Lt.-Col. J. P. Carne, VC during his captivity as a prisoner of war in Korea. It was placed here in 1953 after a thanksgiving service to mark the regiment's safe return to England.

Adjacent to the sixteenth-century effigy of King Osric, founder of the earliest monastery on this site in 679, stands the magnificent tomb of King Edward II who was brutally murdered at Berkeley Castle in 1327. The finely carved oolitic limestone canopy surmounts a tomb chest of

Purbeck marble. The king's effigy is an early use of alabaster and it has been suggested that the face may have been modelled from a death mask. Large niches have been cut away from the Norman pillars at either end of the tomb, possibly to allow access around the tomb for the pilgrims who flocked here to visit the relics of the king. The capitals of the columns are decorated with the badge of Richard II, the white hart, commemorating his stay at the Abbey during the Gloucester Parliament of 1378.

The NORTH TRANSEPT was, like the south transept, altered in the fourteenth century, but its vault is more accomplished and stands some 2.4 m. (8 ft.) higher. On the north side of the transept is the early thirteenth-century structure traditionally known as the reliquary. Although it has stood here since the late fourteenth century its original site is still a mystery. In 1977 an entrance was created through the central arch into the splendid Norman *locutorium*, or talking place, which now houses the CATHEDRAL TREASURY. Exhibited here is the church plate from many parishes throughout the Gloucester diocese.

The art nouveau clock on the west wall was given as a memorial to Canon Bartholomew Price, a notable astronomer, in 1903. The hands of this unusual timepiece were once driven by a series of copper rods and universal joints from the clock in the tower. Below is an unusual early seventeenth-century memorial to surgeon Alderman John Bower depicting him with his wife and their nine sons and seven daughters. From the transept access is gained, via a stairway, to the tribune gallery where there is a permanent exhibition detailing the history of the abbey and cathedral. The chapels in the north and south galleries on either side of the choir are connected by a bridge-passage called the whispering gallery from its ability to transmit a whisper from end to end.

The NORTH AISLE, with the exception of the two western bays, retains the original Norman rib vaults and window openings. These windows have fifteenth-century tracery that is filled mostly with nineteenth-century decorative glass; one scene depicts the martyrdom in 1555 of John Hooper, second bishop of Gloucester. The west window illustrates the life of the second century King Lucius who, allegedly, was buried in the city. Other figures represented are Robert of Normandy and three dukes of Gloucester.

The aisle also contains a variety of memorials to past local worthies. Several members of the bellfounding Rudhall family are commemorated, as is John Stafford Smith, who was an ex-chorister and son of an eighteenth-century cathedral organist. Smith has the distinction of composing the tune now used for the American National Anthem.

The First World War poet and composer Ivor Gurney has a plaque dedicated to his memory sited on a pillar at the eastern end of the nave arcade. While on the north-west wall is the elaborate seventeenth-century monument of John Machen who is depicted wearing his robes of office as Mayor of Gloucester.

The fan tracery of the GREAT CLOISTER is the earliest known example in the country and dates from the second half of the fourteenth century. The south walk of the cloister contains twenty carrels or cubicles used by the monks of the abbey for writing and study. Each carrel was furnished with a desk and a stool, and was separated from its neighbour by a screen or curtain to afford a measure of privacy.

The east walk gives access to the chapter house where in monastic times all matters concerning the daily life of the abbey and its community were discussed. Just to the north of the chapter house is the doorway that led to the domestic quarters and the stairway to the monks' dormitory. At the northern end of the walk is a doorway to the little cloister and the abbey infirmary.

The north walk houses the monks' washing place or *lavatorium* that was supplied with fresh water piped in from a spring on Robinswood Hill. Part of the walk was probably used by the novice monks who whiled away their spare moments here prior to their entry into the rigid discipline of the abbey. The stone bench against the north wall bears scratchings on its surface for the playing of the games Fox and Geese and Nine Men's Morris.

The window at the northern end of the west walk was originally a doorway that gave admittance to the refectory building that ran parallel with the north walk and also to the cellarer's store and the monastic kitchens.

Also in the west walk is a doorway which led to the abbot's lodgings, but today gives access to the cathedral shop and restaurant. The last door at the southern end of the walk leads to the slype or parlour where the brethren were permitted to meet their families and other people from the secular world.

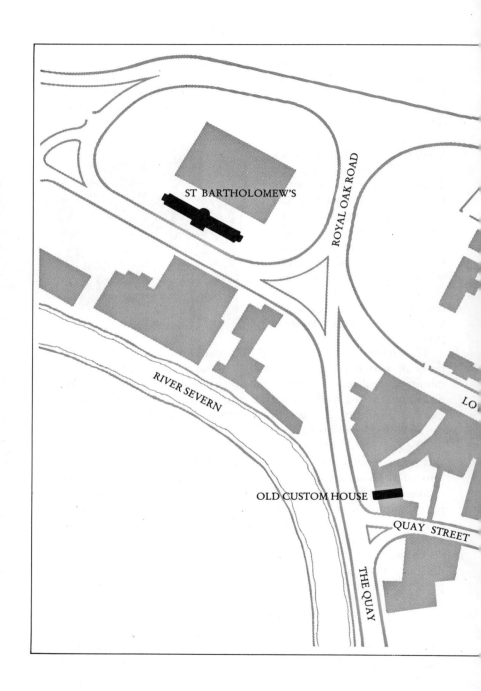

ST BARTHOLOMEW'S

ROYAL OAK ROAD

RIVER SEVERN

LO

OLD CUSTOM HOUSE

QUAY STREET

THE QUAY

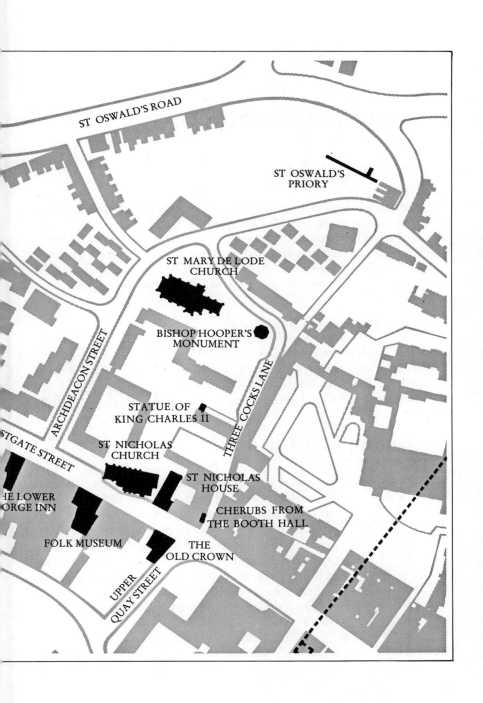

ST OSWALD'S ROAD

ST OSWALD'S
PRIORY

ST MARY DE LODE
CHURCH

BISHOP HOOPER'S
MONUMENT

ARCHDEACON STREET

THREE COCKS LANE

STATUE OF
KING CHARLES II

STGATE STREET

ST NICHOLAS
CHURCH

ST NICHOLAS
HOUSE

HE LOWER
ORGE INN

CHERUBS FROM
THE BOOTH HALL

FOLK MUSEUM

THE
OLD CROWN

UPPER
QUAY STREET

Lower Westgate Street

Three Cocks Lane

The name is derived from an eighteenth-century inn that stood on the western side of the lane near the junction with St Mary's Square. In the early fourteenth century the thoroughfare was known as Abbey Lane for it gave access from Westgate Street to the western gateway in the Abbey precinct wall. By 1649 the title had changed to Portcullis Lane which, like the present name, was also taken from an inn.

Cherubs from the Booth Hall

The city arms were carved in the eighteenth century by Thomas Ricketts to adorn the pediment of the Booth Hall that stood adjacent to the Shire Hall until 1957.

Statue of King Charles II

The statue was first set up at the northern end of the Wheat Market in Southgate Street in 1662 as part of the city's political rehabilitation following the restoration of the monarchy. A pledge of allegiance given to the king by the men of Gloucester was graciously accepted but Charles, no doubt mindful of the city's recent pro-parliamentarian sympathies, and the part it played in the downfall of his father, returned the compliment by ordering the demolition of the City walls.

The king's effigy was removed and ultimately lost when the Wheat Market was taken down in the eighteenth century. It was rediscovered in a garden at Chaxhill near Westbury-on-Severn in 1945 and erected here in the 1960s.

Humpty Dumpty

The original version of the well-known nursery rhyme has been traced back to the Siege of Gloucester in 1643. The subject of the verse was, in fact, a siege-engine designed by Dr Chillingworth that was used to attack the defences of the parliamentarian garrison. However the machines were rendered useless when they fell over and stuck fast in the soggy mire of the city ditch. At the raising of the siege the engines were trundled into Gloucester in triumph by the jubilant citizens.

> Humpty Dumpty fell in a beck
> With all his sinews around his neck
> Forty surgeons and Forty knights
> Couldn't put Humpty Dumpty to rights.

This episode in Gloucester's history is featured in an operetta by Richard Rodney Bennett entitled *All the King's Men*.

Bishop Hooper's Monument

The monument to the protestant martyr was erected in 1862 to mark the site of his execution by fire in 1555. During the excavations for the foundations of the memorial the stump of a charred wooden stake was discovered.

Bishop John Hooper

The second bishop of Gloucester was born in 1495 in Somerset, the son of well-to-do parents. On completion of his education at Merton College, Oxford, he is believed to have become a monk at the Cistercian monastery at Cleeve, and later a friar at Blackfriars in Gloucester. After the dissolution of the monasteries he returned to Oxford where, much to the disapproval of the Regius Professor of Divinity, Dr Smith, he became greatly influenced by the extreme Protestant reformers Bullinger and Zwingli. His forthright opinions against the established practice of the church led to a severe admonishment from Bishop Gardiner of Winchester and ultimately caused him to flee to the Continent in 1539. Hooper settled in Zurich for two or three years following his marriage to Anne de Tserclas of Antwerp in 1546. They had two children, Rachel and Daniel.

In 1547 Henry VIII died and was succeeded by the nine-year-old Edward VI who ruled England under the watchful eye of the Duke of Somerset, Protector of the Realm, and strong advocate of religious reform. On Hooper's return to his native country he was appointed personal chaplain to the duke and later preached at the royal court. In his first sermon he denounced as blasphemy the Oath of Supremacy which required men to swear by the saints as well as God and also described the sumptuous priestly garments worn at church services as superstitious and anti-Christian. Despite the reservations of Archbishop Cranmer, the king was impressed by the preacher and offered him the vacant see of Gloucester. Initially Hooper refused the appointment claiming that there were elements of Popery in the induction ceremony, but after two weeks of contemplation in the Fleet Prison he changed his mind.

He was consecrated Bishop of Gloucester on 8 March 1551. On arrival at the city he made a thorough visitation of his see and examined the clergy in their knowledge of the Ten Commandments, the Apostles' Creed and the Lord's Prayer. Of 311 clergy examined, 171 could not repeat the Ten Commandments; 10 were unable to recite the Lord's Prayer and 27 did not know its author. The minister of Tewkesbury parish church was found to be 'a man of remarkable learning' but the vicar of Frampton-on-Severn was 'entirely ignorant'. In order to correct this poor state of affairs the bishop drew up a list of fifty articles to be observed by all the incumbents. The severe disciplinary regime he imposed at Gloucester led to him being called a tyrant and a beast.

Edward VI died on 6 July 1553 and was succeeded by his sister Mary, a devout Catholic who was determined to stamp out protestantism. During her five years' reign she was responsible for the deaths of nearly three hundred 'heretics' which earned her the title 'Bloody Mary'.

Hooper was summoned to appear before the new Queen's Council to answer a false charge of misappropriation of funds from the Gloucester see. He was sent to the Fleet Prison where he was kept in appalling conditions for over a year. Following further theological inquisition he was moved to Newgate Prison where, in the chapel, he was degraded from the priesthood and informed of his impending execution by fire at Gloucester, the scene of his purported heresy.

Hooper arrived back in the city in the charge of six armed guards and on 8 February 1555 lodged at the house of Robert Ingram, opposite the steeple of St Nicholas church, in Westgate Street. At nine o'clock the following morning John Hooper was taken to the place of execution just to the east of St Mary de Lode church where a crowd of over seven thousand had assembled. He was bound to the wooden stake by an iron hoop and spent time supervising the placement of the bundles of reeds around his legs. The fire was lit but the reeds merely smouldered. The fire was lit again but it managed only to burn his hair and scorch his skin a little before it was blown out by the wind. Hooper chided his executioners with the words 'For the love of God, friends, give me more fire.' Dry wood was brought and heaped around him, and for good measure three bags of gun powder were tied around his body. The fire was lit for the last time and he was engulfed in flames, but the ordeal was to last for three-quarters of an hour. The gun powder had been badly placed and he remained fully conscious. An eye witness described the final moments of the Protestant martyr:

> ... but when he was black in the mouth and his tongue swollen, that he could not speak, yet his lips went till they were shrunk to the gums, and he knocked his breast with his hands until one of his arms fell off, and then knocked still with the other, what time the fat, water and blood, dropped at his finger ends, until by renewing of the fire his strength was gone and his hand did cleave fast in knocking to the iron upon his breast. So, immediately bowing forwards, he yielded up his spirit.

It is prophetic that when John Hooper was consecrated second Bishop of Gloucester he had chosen for his coat of arms the lamb in the burning bush.

St Mary de Lode Church

The word Lode is derived from the Old English 'lad' meaning a watercourse or a ford through it and, in this case, refers to a ferry or bridge that once crossed the now vanished third arm of the River Severn that flowed just to the west of the church.

St Mary de Lode is generally held to be the city's oldest parish church. According to local tradition, it was the burial place of Lucius, who, it is said, was a king of Britain who established a bishopric in Gloucester in the second century. Bede relates that Lucius was converted

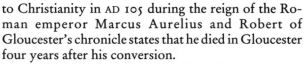

to Christianity in AD 105 during the reign of the Roman emperor Marcus Aurelius and Robert of Gloucester's chronicle states that he died in Gloucester four years after his conversion.

The findings from an archaeological excavation in the nave in 1979 suggest the presence of a church here since Saxon times or even earlier, and it may be be significant that these features overlie the remains of a Roman building.

The earliest church mentioned in written records belongs to the late eleventh or early twelfth century. It consisted of a chancel, nave and a central tower that was later destroyed by fire in 1190. The present chancel was constructed in the thirteenth century together with the addition of side aisles to the nave.

Two chantries were established within the church; the first in the early fourteenth century was dedicated to St Mary and the second was founded by the religious guild of Holy Trinity in 1420.

In March 1643 the church was used briefly as a prison to hold some of the 1500 royalist soldiers captured at Highnam by Sir William Waller and Lieutenant Colonel Massey. Most were held for ten days then released on the condition that they would not fight against Parliament again. A lengthy detention of these men would have been a severe strain on the city's food resources, as it was they were fed only turnip tops and cabbage leaves. The church served the same purpose again in 1646 when captives from Stow-on-the-Wold were brought to Gloucester.

The NAVE of the church was rebuilt in 1826 in the Early Gothic Revival style. It is much broader than its medieval predecessor and the roof span is supported on rows of iron columns. The nave contains a fifteenth-century wooden PULPIT restored with old gothic panels; the eighteenth-century ORGAN was installed here in 1971 following its removal from nearby St Nicholas church.

The central Norman TOWER is finished with an open work parapet and pinnacles at each corner. It carried a spire until the early eighteenth century when this was blown down in a violent storm. The tower houses a ring of six bells, four of which were cast by the famous Gloucester bell founder, Abraham Rudhall. The western arch of the tower is Norman with restored chevron ornament. The eastern arch belongs to the thirteenth century and has foliate capitals and plain roll moulding.

The EAST WINDOW of the CHANCEL has three lights that were inserted in the nineteenth century. On the north wall is an early fourteenth-century arched recess that contains St Mary de Lode's most notable monument. It is an effigy of a priest in eucharistic vestments which is said to be of William de Chamberlain who died in 1304.

St Oswald's Priory

Following the Battle of Maser-field in 641 the body of St Oswald of Northumbria, king and martyr, was dismembered and hung on poles by the victorious pagan King Penda. Later, the head of the saint was interred at Lindisfarne and his right arm at Bamburgh. Osthryth, his niece, collected the other remains and interred them at Bardney in Lincolnshire. In 909 these remains were seized from Bardney and brought to Gloucester where they were placed in the new minster church founded by Aethelflaeda, daughter of Alfred the Great, and her husband Aethelred, Lord of the Mercians. The shrine they created became a major place of pilgrimage for people seeking the cures that the saint's relics were believed to bring.

Aethelflaeda died at Tamworth in June 918 and was buried, like her husband Aethelred, at Gloucester; almost certainly at St Oswald's. During the course of an archaeological excavation at the priory in the 1970s a fragment of an intricately carved stone grave-slab was un-earthed. It dates from the early tenth century and obviously belonged to a person of very high rank.

The church was enlarged in the twelfth century and was remodelled as a house of Augustinian canons by Archbishop Henry Murdac in 1153.

After the Norman Conquest the importance of St Oswald's gradu-ally declined especially after the royal palace at nearby Kingsholm was abandoned in favour of the newly built castle in the south-western corner of the town. The lands and jurisdiction of the minster fell into the hands of the archbishops of York who were in acrimonious dispute over their possession with Worcester and Canterbury for the next two centuries. The Bishop of Worcester even went as far as excommunicating all canons of St Oswald's and he forbade the towns-people of Gloucester to sell them food. The ban was finally lifted by Edward I who claimed that St Oswald's was a Royal Free Chapel and, as such, was immune from the bishop's jurisdiction.

When the priory was finally dissolved by King Henry VIII there remained only seven serving canons and their eight servants. The north aisle of the church was converted into the parish church, dedicated to St Catherine, which, in 1548, was attended by some three hundred communicants. The parish church was largely destroyed by Royalist canon fire during the Civil War and much of the fabric was used in building a new market house in Eastgate Street in 1655. From the seventeenth century the parish was without a place of worship until a new church was built adjacent to the ruins in 1868. This in turn was demolished in the early twentieth century and replaced by a new building at Wotton in 1915.

The surviving structure is part of the north arcade of the nave of the priory church, and probably owes its survival to the series of outhouses and sheds that were built against it following the destruction of the seventeenth century.

The large stone blocks in the upper part of the arcade belong to the north wall of Aethelflaeda's tenth-century church which measures 8.5 m. (28 ft.) in width and has a conjectured length of some 23 m. (75 ft.). It had a north and south porticus and an apse at its western end.

The four round arches date from the addition of a north aisle in the twelfth century. The two pointed arches at the eastern end form part of an extension to the nave carried out in the thirteenth century. The blocking of these two arches together with two of the twelfth-century arches dates from the conversions of the north aisle into the parish church of St Catherine in the sixteenth century.

The Old Crown

The Old Crown Inn was re-established in Westgate Street in 1990 by Samuel Smith's Brewery exactly 230 years after the original inn closed down. From the 1400s the Crown Inn occupied a large parcel of land fronting onto part of Upper Quay Street and onto Westgate Street as far down as No. 91. The hostelry co-existed on the site alongside other trades such as a blacksmith, a saddler and a baker.

The name of the inn was changed briefly to The Tabard in the early seventeenth century but had reverted to The Crown under the tenure of Thomas Hale, a Sergeant at Arms to King James I. It is ironic that the hostelry was later used as a lodging house and centre of operations by the military governor of Gloucester, Lieutenant-Colonel Edward Massey, whilst directing the city's resistance to the Stuart cause during the English Civil War. Certainly the Royalist battery at Llanthony had the building in the sights of their culverin during the Siege of Gloucester in 1643. A contemporary account relates: 'one bullet of about twenty pound in weight came through a chamber of the inne called the Crowne, carried a boulster before it into a window and there slept in it.'

By 1680 the inn had adopted the style 'old' following the estab- lishment of another public house called the Crown in the southern part of the city. In 1730 the inn was up- graded by the addition of a new façade and the refurbishment of the courtyard and stables. It became the recognised point of departure for the carrier's wagon that transported goods between Gloucester and Ross, Hereford and Monmouth; an opera-  tion that was seemingly conducted in a leisurely manner for the operator arrived in the city on Mondays and departed 'the same week'. The Old Crown became the venue for many activities and meetings; at Christmas 1744 it was used as a recruiting office by Corporal George Miller in his search for likely candidates to serve as troopers in His Majesty's Own Regiment.

By October 1760 the inn had ceased trading and the stables had been converted into workshops and stores by an eminent local wine merchant Alderman Benjamin Saunders, Mayor of Gloucester in 1745 and 1756. The gentle aromas of beer and wine were finally banished from the premises by Alderman Saunders' son Thomas, who later occupied the workshops in his capacity as a tallow chandler and soap boiler.

Lieutenant-Colonel Edward Massey

Edward Massey was a professional soldier and engineer who fought in Holland and with Charles I in the Scottish campaigns of 1640. At the outbreak of the English Civil War he applied for, and was refused, a commission in the king's army; he later joined the parliamentary cause as a lieutenant-colonel under the Earl of Stamford. In 1643, at the age of twenty-three, he was appointed Governor of Gloucester and commander of the city garrison which amounted to 1500 men. Massey distinguished himself not only for the spirited defence of

Gloucester against a royalist force of up to 30,000 troops, but also for his brilliant military forays in the ensuing months. Despite these successes he was always dogged by the lack of money and men, and the undermining of his authority by city officials.

Edward Massey left Gloucester in 1645 and became MP for Wotton Bassett and soon found himself embroiled with the religious factions that controlled Parliament and the new model army. Following his refusal to help raise an army for the defence of London he was impeached and fled to Holland. On his return he was banned from Parliament and imprisoned but later escaped to the Continent.

Disenchanted with the parliamentary cause Massey offered his services to Charles II and fought in the Scottish Campaign in 1649. He was badly wounded at Upton-on-Severn prior to the Battle of Worcester and was taken into custody but managed to escape. On his recapture he was imprisoned in the Tower of London but escaped again and fled to France. At the restoration Massey returned to Gloucester in April 1660 and despite the objections of some of the inhabitants, he was elected MP. Later he was knighted by Charles II and appointed Governor of Jamaica.

100 Westgate Street, St Nicholas House

This building was used as a town house by the Whittington family who owned the manor and estates at Pauntley, near Newent, from 1311 to 1546. In 1455 the house was occupied by Richard Whittington, Lord of Staunton, who was probably the son of Robert of Pauntley, the brother of the famous Dick Whittington. The nearby Gloucester Folk Museum has, amongst its collections, a piece of stonework which has a relief carving of a young boy holding a cat in his arms. This stone, thought to be part of a fifteenth-century chimney piece, is said to have been found, in 1862, in the course of repairs to St Nicholas House.

Dick Whittington was born in the 1350s, the third son of William Whittington, Lord of Pauntley. At the age of thirteen he was sent to London to be apprenticed to John Fitzwaryn a merchant banker and a close family friend. On completion of his apprenticeship, the young Dick proved to be an astute businessman and eventually became the greatest merchant in medieval England. He was court mercer and supplied material, including silks from Peking, for the wedding gowns for the daughters of Henry IV; he also lent money to the crown to pay for foreign wars and generally made himself indispensable to the king and State. He became Mayor of London four times in the years 1397, 1398, 1407 and 1420, and amassed a considerable fortune; and true to the pantomime story, he did indeed marry the boss's daughter, Alice.

As to the famous cat, we shall probably never know how much of the tale is fact or fiction. However, Whittington built the church of St Michael Royal (or St Michael Paternoster) in London, which became his regular place of worship and where he and his wife are buried. During the Great Fire of London in 1666, this church was burnt, but was rebuilt in 1694 by Sir Christopher Wren's master mason, Edward Strong. In 1944, during World War II it was damaged by bombs, and workmen carrying out repairs to the tower discovered the mummified body of a cat.

According to local legend St Nicholas House ranks alongside countless others in England as being one of the places where Queen Elizabeth I slept. She is said to have held court here following her arrival in Gloucester on the 8 August 1574. The house has a large room that once contained a finely carved fireplace and pretentious overmantel bearing the royal coat of arms of Elizabeth I. The entire room was walled with wooden panelling with a carved frieze at ceiling level and around the doorways. This was sold together with the fireplace for £750 in 1907 and is now believed to be in Chicago, USA.

A notable lessee of the house in the early seventeenth century was John Taylor. As a member of the Common Council of Gloucester he was severely censured by his fellow councillors when, in April 1604, he concealed the fact that one of his servants lay dead of the plague and another had plague boils under his arms while, at the same time, the mayor and aldermen were being entertained in his house. Taylor was immediately expelled from the council and ordered to pay £100 for the relief of those who had been infected as a result of his dishonest actions.

All the members of his family were ordered to stay inside the house and the front door was boarded up. Taylor's son, also called John, took exception to this and broke down the door threatening to shoot the men guarding the property. For this action and for making some extremely rude remarks about the mayor, he was fined 100 marks (£67) and ordered to be put in the stocks in Southgate Street on three separate market days.

Despite having been imprisoned several times and disenfranchised four times, John Taylor senior became Mayor of Gloucester in 1613. He was, however, removed from office accused of embezzlement, receiving bribes, extortion, drunkenness and for refusing to swear in the newly-elected Town Clerk.

The early eighteenth-century façade onto Westgate Street is a good example of Georgian provincial architecture and may have been added during the tenure of James Pitt who was the licensee of The King's Head Inn, one of the largest and most important inns in Gloucester at the time and which adjoined this property on the eastern side.

In 1822 the dean and chapter of Gloucester Cathedral granted a dispensation to the tenant John Powell to allow the house to be used for public worship by Protestant Dissenters. As a result of this the property was renamed Church Court and remained as such until 1846.

During the restoration of St Nicholas House in the 1970s an exuberant floral wall-painting was discovered behind wainscoting in a room at the northern end of the building. This wall painting, possibly dating from the sixteenth century, was preserved, together with other historic features, when the building was converted into a restaurant.

St Nicholas Church

The parish of St Nicholas was established before the end of the twelfth century and by 1203 the church was called St Nicholas of the Bridge at Gloucester, indicating that it had custody of the new bridge built across the Severn in the preceding century. The parish was one of the largest and most prosperous in the city and contained part of the medieval quayside area on the now vanished third arm of the river. Its maritime connections may be reflected in the church's dedication, as St Nicholas is the patron saint of sailors, as well as dockers and fishermen.

Although the church was rebuilt and enlarged in the thirteenth century, part of the earlier fabric still survives in the form of the carved tympanum above the SOUTH DOORWAY and the round arches on fat cylindrical Norman pillars at the western end of the north arcade of the nave.

The Royal Coat of Arms set above the south door at the western end of the nave were first installed in 1665 during the reign of Charles II but were removed in the reign of his papist brother James. In 1689, following the accession of William and Mary, the arms were restored to the church in an altered form.

A gallery was built at the western end of the church in the Jacobean period and occupied the area west of the south doorway. The gallery was later truncated and placed under the tower and, despite its eventual removal in 1924, part of the carved oak panelled front still survives within the church.

The NORTH AISLE was reconstructed and extended in the early fifteenth century and rebuilt again in 1935. The larger SOUTH AISLE functioned as a chapel dedicated to St Mary in the fourteenth century and the windows facing onto Westgate Street were inserted in the fifteenth century.

Quadruple squints were built into the side walls of the chancel in the sixteenth century to afford the congregation in the north and south aisles a view of the proceedings at the altar.

The church contains an interesting collection of funerary monuments and floor slabs that illustrate the diversity of trades and professions within the parish during the seventeenth and eighteenth centuries. Several memorials are dedicated to mayors and aldermen of the city, for indeed the church of St Nicholas was used by the mayor and corporation for civic services between 1738 and 1751 as the result of a dispute with the dean and chapter over the seating arrangements in the cathedral.

The finest MONUMENTS in the church are to be found at its eastern end. In the south aisle stands a seventeenth-century tomb-chest with the painted stone effigies of Alderman John Wallton and his wife Alice dressed in contemporary costume. Another fine memorial is set into the south wall of the chancel and is dedicated to the memory of the Rev. Richard Green, MA who died in 1711, aged twenty-three. He had the distinction of penning his own funeral sermon.

The superb WEST TOWER, built in the early fifteenth century, is decorated with ogee hood mouldings and blank arcading which until 1969 was finished with a traceried and battlemented parapet. The spire originally soared to over 61 m. (200 ft.) in height but the uppermost part suffered a direct hit from Royalist artillery during the Siege of Gloucester in 1643. Although the damage was repaired, the structure eventually became unstable and in 1783 it was shortened to about half its original height. The tower leans considerably to the north-east and close inspection will reveal that it began moving whilst under construction as the vertical line of the upper stage was corrected to allow for the tilt. The original wooden bell frame in the tower supports a ring of six bells that are still occasionally rung on St Nicholas day in December.

The CLOCK was installed shortly after 1700, probably with a single dial affixed to the south face of the tower, but by 1790 it had been converted into the twin dial arrangement we see today. The hands are now driven by an electric motor housed in the ringing chamber which still contains much of the original clock mechanism together with the remnants of a carillon.

The church passed into the care of the Redundant Churches Fund in 1975 following the unification of the congregation of St Nicholas with that of St Mary de Lode. The building is still occasionally used for concerts and exhibitions.

99-103 Westgate Street, Gloucester Folk Museum

The Folk Museum was established following the purchase and restoration of 99-101 Westgate Street by the Gloucester Corporation in 1933.

In 1548 the property was owned by a wealthy clothier, John Sandford, who probably used the extensive accommodation for the storage of cloth. At this time the façade of the first floor possessed a continuous row of leaded lights that would have provided ideal conditions for the needlework entailed in the manufacture of the garments that were offered for sale in the shop below.

Local tradition asserts that Bishop John Hooper lodged at No. 101 prior to his execution in St Mary's Square in 1555. He is known to have stayed at a house opposite the steeple of St Nicholas Church. By 1743 the premises were occupied by William Coucher who established a pin manufactory on the upper floor of No. 91. This continued in operation until 1853.

Pinmakers are first mentioned in Gloucester in 1396, working from small workshops in back yards and on the upper floors of houses. The industry expanded in the late seventeenth century following encouragement and incentives from the mayor and burgesses of the city

together with a plentiful supply of cheap labour. By 1744 pinmaking had become a major industry in Gloucester which, by 1802, employed one in five of the inhabitants at nine manufactories.

In the eighteenth century one pinmaker set up his factory at the City Workhouse in Bearland where the inmates were taught the various processes of manufacture. Women and children were employed mainly in heading pins and sticking them on cards ready for sale. The children received no payment during the first six months of their employment but received thereafter the princely sum of 1¼d. for every 12,000 pins they handled. The women, however, fared better for they received 2d. The generous master also provided candles during the dark winter days but the fuel for the hearths was provided by the workhouse guardians.

No. 103 Westgate Street dates from about 1640 and is partly timber-framed. From 1950 until 1978 it housed the Museum of the Gloucestershire Regiment. Today the museum contains many fascinating displays including a dairy, shoemaker's and carpenter's workshops, an ironmonger's shop and a very popular Victorian schoolroom as well as agricultural, folklife, and fishery exhibits.

121 Westgate Street, The Lower George Inn

An inn sign has hung from this building since the early sixteenth century when it originally featured Saint George, the patron saint of England. 'Lower' was added to the name in the eighteenth century in order to distinguish it from the Upper George Inn that stood further up Westgate Street.

The Lower George ranked among the chief inns in Gloucester specialising in providing accommodation for travelling salesmen. One regular visitor in the 1730s was a Mr Duckett of Fairford who toured the county peddling his cures for deafness. The inn was upgraded in the early nineteenth century by the addition of a new façade. By 1822 it was one of the five establishments in the city operating stagecoaches. It was also known at this time as a fashionable residential hotel and a much favoured venue for meetings.

John Taylor, the Water Poet

The earliest of the Gloucester poets, John Taylor, was born of humble parentage on 24 August 1580. On completion of his education at the Crypt Grammar School he was apprenticed to a London waterman and was subsequently press-ganged into the navy to serve under the Earl of Essex. He later supplemented his meagre living as a waterman by utilising his talent for composing easy rhymes. Taylor was always ready, on reasonable terms and at short notice, to provide a suitable rhyme for a birthday, a wedding or a funeral.

He also started to travel and issued a vast number of notices or 'Taylor's bills' as he called them, describing the journey to be undertaken in the hope of attracting sponsors who would ultimately receive a printed account of the excursion. In this way he travelled to Bohemia, Germany, Scotland and Wales. One of the more bizarre journeys undertaken by Taylor, in the company of a friend, was a voyage from London to Queenborough in Kent in a brown-paper boat propelled by two stockfish tied to canes. Not surprisingly the boat began to disintegrate after the first three miles, but the voyage was successfully completed a day and a half later.

In 1613 Taylor was commissioned to arrange a water pageant on the Thames to celebrate the marriage of Elizabeth, sister of Charles I, to Frederic of Bavaria; and again in 1641 to welcome Charles on his return from Scotland.

At the outbreak of Civil War he moved to Oxford where he took a public house and served the royal cause by penning lampoons against the parliamentarians. For this service the king made him a Yeoman of the Guard. With the surrender of Oxford in 1645 he moved back to London where he took another public house called The Crown in Phoenix Alley. After Charles I's execution in 1649 he altered the pub name to The Mourning Crown and for this action he was declared a 'malignant' by parliament so he hung up his own portrait and re-christened the pub The Poet's Head with this description under the sign,

> There's many a head stands for a sign
> Then, gentle Reader, why not mine.

Taylor revisited Gloucester in August 1652 during the course of his last journey and lodged with his namesake the landlord of the Lower George Inn, where, according to his journal, he was disappointed at knowing so few people in his native city. He died in December of the following year, aged seventy-three, and was buried in the churchyard of St Martin-in-the-Fields. His widow Alice continued to run The Poet's Head until her own death in January 1658.

Taylor had, in all, sixty-three published works of poetry and prose containing 141 individual items.

St Bartholomew's Hospital

The origins of this hospital lie in the twelfth century during the reign of Henry II when William Myparty, a burgess of Gloucester, built a house on the site to accommodate the workmen engaged in the construction of a new bridge across the River Severn at the western approaches to the town. On completion of the bridge the house became a hospice for the sick and a shelter for travellers, under the charge of a priest.

In 1229 Henry III gave the church of St Nicholas to the house which then became known as the Hospice of St Bartholomew the Apostle,

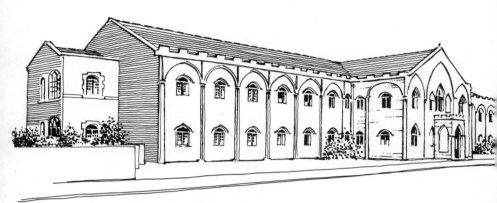

that was charged with the upkeep of the bridge through the collection of tolls. Both the bridge and hospital became ruinous in the late thirteenth century due to the depredations of the Barons' War, and the king was petitioned to fund the necessary repairs. At this time the hospital accommodated ninety sick persons, twelve brethren as well as sisters and lay brothers.

By the sixteenth century St Bartholomews had become the largest and wealthiest of the three ancient hospitals in Gloucester, supporting a master, five priests and thirty-two almspeople from its extensive endowments and property holdings. Following the conveyance of the hospital into the hands of the corporation in 1564 much of the accommodation for the forty almspeople was rebuilt and improved. By 1636 it housed twenty men and thirty women, who each received a weekly allowance of 2s.6d. (12½p.). On admittance to the almshouse an inmate had to provide a bed with bedding, cooking and eating utensils plus a table cloth, three towels and napkins. The community included a physician, a surgeon, a porter, a bellringer, a beadle and a minister responsible for conducting the regular mandatory services in the hospital chapel. In 1786 the resident congregation was treated to a fiery sermon by John Wesley in the course of one of his regular visits to Gloucester.

By 1789 the building had fallen into disrepair and was unsuitable for the needs of the fifty or so residents, so a decision was taken by the corporation to demolish and replace the old building. A local architect, William Price, designed the Gothick-style building that stands today; although it is now devoid of its original small bell-tower and numerous chimney stacks. The new building provided each almsperson with their own apartment containing a bed and a grate; also they each received a garden plot. The new semi-circular chapel

on the northern side was consecrated by the bishop of Gloucester on
1 October 1790.

In 1890 St Bartholomews was incorporated with the United Hospitals, which comprised the other two ancient almshouses St Mary
Magdalen and St Margaret, both in London Road, and administered
by the Gloucester Municipal Charities.

The Westgate property was finally sold by the trustees of the
charity in 1971 and the building was restored and re-opened as a
shopping centre in the 1980s.

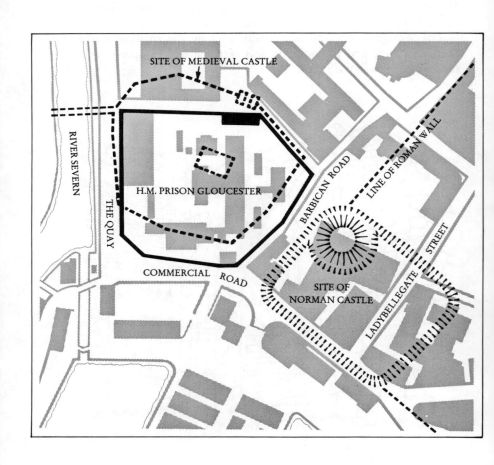

SITE OF MEDIEVAL CASTLE

RIVER SEVERN

THE QUAY

H.M. PRISON GLOUCESTER

COMMERCIAL ROAD

BARBICAN ROAD

LINE OF ROMAN WALL

LADYBELLEGATE STREET

SITE OF NORMAN CASTLE

Castles and County Gaol

The Norman Castle

In 1066 William, Duke of Normandy, launched a successful bid to gain the English throne. The indigenous Anglo-Saxon nobility were ruthlessly deprived of their lands which the Conqueror redistributed amongst his loyal supporters thereby creating a powerful political and military regime. The ultimate symbols of the new armed authority were the hastily constructed castles placed within the existing Saxon townships. The stronghold at Gloucester was sited in the south-west corner of the town and necessitated the demolition of sixteen Saxon dwellings in an area bounded today by Barbican Road and Commercial Road. This early motte-and-bailey castle utilised part of the remaining Roman defences and consisted of a mound of tightly compacted soil topped with a wooden tower to provide a high vantage point and last refuge for the occupants. A further defended enclosure, or bailey, was placed on the eastern side of the motte protected by a ditch and timber palisade with a fortified gateway and drawbridge.

The castle controlled not only the town and its river crossing but also the whole of the surrounding countryside, thus reinforcing the power of its first constable, Roger de Pistres, in his duties as Sheriff of Gloucestershire and collector of the king's revenue.

A glimpse into the life of this early castle was gained during an archaeological excavation in 1983 at 28-32 Commercial Road. The dig revealed a series of eleventh-century timber structures and rubbish pits associated with the bailey enclosure. Discovered at the bottom of one pit were the remains of a tabula or gaming board complete with its set of thirty playing counters. This board, used for an early form of backgammon, is made up of thin bone overlay panels decorated with geometric designs, hunting scenes, dragons and serpents; the counters display a variety of different themes including animals, biblical scenes and astrological signs. The board had been deliberately smashed before its consignment into the pit, suggesting perhaps that a member of the constable's household may have been a poor loser or that it was a gesture by someone attempting to forsake the evils of gambling. The latter is unlikely however as the dice have never been

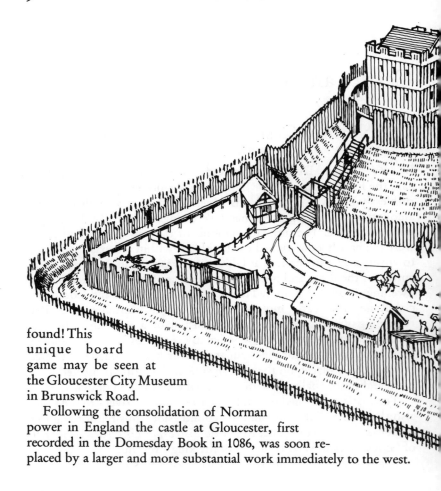

found! This
unique board
game may be seen at
the Gloucester City Museum
in Brunswick Road.

Following the consolidation of Norman
power in England the castle at Gloucester, first
recorded in the Domesday Book in 1086, was soon replaced by a larger and more substantial work immediately to the west.

The Medieval Castle

The new castle was raised by Walter, son of Roger de Pistres, probably
during the second decade of the twelfth century, on land between the
old castle and the River Severn acquired by Henry I from St Peter's
Abbey. The tall central tower, or keep, was enclosed with stone walls
12.2 m. (40 ft.) high and 1.83 m. (6 ft.) thick, defended by water-filled
ditches connected to the river on the western side. Access to the
castle's main gate was from Westgate Street via Castle Lane (Upper
Quay Street); lesser gates were sited in the south and west walls, the

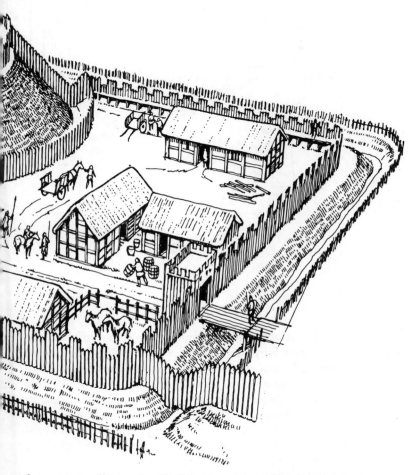

latter controlling a fortified bridge that spanned the river. Walter's castle occupied much of the area that is today enclosed by the perimeter walls of Gloucester Gaol.

The castle at Gloucester was originally held by the earls of Hereford but following the rebellion of Earl Roger against King Stephen in 1155 it passed into the hands of the crown. It become a principal stronghold in the west of England, functioning as a military base and mustering point for various royal armies. Henry II assembled and

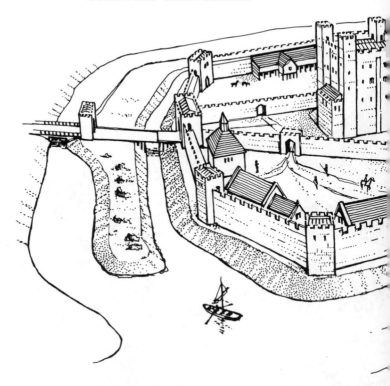

provisioned his forces here prior to the Irish expedition in 1171. The Welsh campaign against Rhys ap Gryffudd, early in the reign of Richard I, was also launched from within its lofty walls. Queen Isabella of Angoulême, the adulterous second wife of John, was imprisoned within these same walls in 1214 after the king had allegedly 'hanged her gallants above her bed'. She remained here until his death two years later.

The castle became a favoured royal residence following the coronation of Henry III at Gloucester in 1216. During the first half of the thirteenth century the king embarked upon a series of improvements by erecting free-standing buildings containing suites of rooms for Queen Eleanor and Prince Edward. He also made alterations to the keep, great hall, buttery and kitchen, thus creating a place of great comfort and architectural splendour set amidst pleasant gardens and meadows on the banks of the Severn.

Henry was a weak and untrustworthy king, who raised the ire of the barons by installing many of his wife's French relatives in positions of importance. The appointment of Matthew de Besille as constable of Gloucester and sheriff of the county in 1263, was

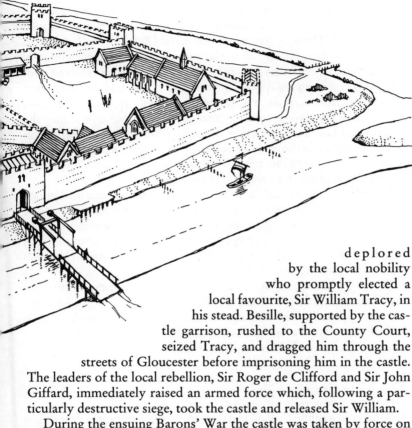

deplored
by the local nobility
who promptly elected a
local favourite, Sir William Tracy, in
his stead. Besille, supported by the castle garrison, rushed to the County Court,
seized Tracy, and dragged him through the
streets of Gloucester before imprisoning him in the castle.
The leaders of the local rebellion, Sir Roger de Clifford and Sir John
Giffard, immediately raised an armed force which, following a particularly destructive siege, took the castle and released Sir William.

During the ensuing Barons' War the castle was taken by force on
two other occasions and the town of Gloucester was pillaged by
Prince Edward's army. King Henry was eventually captured by
Simon de Montfort and had the ignominy of being held prisoner in
his own castle at Gloucester.

By the fourteenth century the fabric of the building was in serious
decline and it was no longer fit for use as a royal residence. Richard II
when attending the Gloucester Parliament of 1378 elected to stay as
a guest at St Peter's Abbey. From the reign of Richard III the defensive
outer walls of the castle became a quarry for building stone and the
keep and main gatehouse were consigned to the role of county prison.
Despite the building of a new bridewell in the 1640s the castle became
ruinous by the end of the century. Its decay was so far advanced by
the second half of the eighteenth century that it became of prime
concern to local social reformers.

When John Howard published his *State of Prisons in England and Wales* in 1777 he included a shocking description of the county gaol at Gloucester. The only day room measured 3.6 x 3 metres (12 ft. x 10 ft.) which was occupied by up to sixty-five prisoners indiscriminately herded together regardless of age, sex or offence. Felons received a 6d. (2½p.) loaf every two days but debtors had no such allowance, often being saved from starvation by other inmates who shared their rations with them. The gaoler received £10 per annum for overseeing the bridewell, a house of correction for petty offenders, but received no salary for duties in the main gaol. His chief income was derived from the sale of beer to the inmates who obtained money from a levy called 'garnish' placed on all newcomers to the gaol.

There were no medical facilities, no baths and only one inadequate sewer that led to the creation of a large dunghill at the entrance to one of the staircases. These appalling conditions left the inmates prey to the scourge of gaol-fever, an epidemic typhus disease common to all prisons at this time. In Gloucestershire three times as many prisoners died from the fever as were hanged on the gallows.

In 1783 a leading county magistrate Sir George Onesiphorus Paul urged the rebuilding of the gaol along the lines advocated by the reformer John Howard. Subsequently an Act empowering the county authorities to build a new gaol was passed in 1785, and the demolition of the medieval castle keep began in 1787.

The New County Gaol

Sir George Onesiphorus Paul had the good fortune to engage the services of William Blackburn, an award-winning designer in the then new art of purpose-built prisons. The structure he created suited the three main principles of reform championed by Paul namely Health, Security and, where appropriate, Separation. The extensive three-storey buildings were arranged around three courtyards to provide accommodation for up to 207 inmates segregated according to sex, age and nature of offence. The cell blocks were sited well above ground to provide a plentiful supply of fresh air, indeed, all the floors, ceilings and walls were liberally peppered with iron grills to encourage a high volume of ventilation.

A revolutionary feature incorporated into the new county gaol was the first lazaretto or entrance lodge built at a distance from the the the main complex. Here the new arrivals received a bath, a health check and had their clothes fumigated to ensure that no unhealthy prisoner was introduced into the closed community.

The new model gaol with its recently completed high security perimeter wall came into
operation on the last Friday in July 1791 even
though a certain amount of building work
remained to be done. In the following October a William Nichols, incarcerated for stealing a shirt, took full advantage of a builder's
ladder to make history as the first escapee.
Shortly afterwards John Cull effected an
identical breakout but was brought back the
next day by his irate wife to complete the rest of his two-year sentence.
Several ingenious and daring escapes took place in the following years
but the fears of officials that prisoners would escape via ropes thrown
into the prison from ships moored at the adjacent quayside proved
unfounded.

The flat roof of the entrance lodge provided a new platform upon
which to carry out the hanging of convicted felons, a practice which
in previous years had taken place on a piece of ground near Over
Bridge just to the west of the city. The first execution at the new gaol
took place on 14 April 1792 following Charles Rackford's conviction
for highway robbery. The record number of hangings on any one day
at Gloucester occurred on 18 April 1818 when three sheep stealers, a
rapist and a housebreaker were dispatched above the gate and a robber
was hanged at the city prison that stood near Kimbrose Way. One
fleet-footed observer stated that he had witnessed all six hangings 'and
all afore breakfast'. A very sad incident occurred in 1811 when
William Townley was executed for burglary despite a reprieve being
despatched from Hereford the previous evening. The letter had been
wrongly addressed to the under Sheriff of Herefordshire when it
should have read Gloucestershire. It was immediately redirected by
express post but arrived twenty minutes too late.

Over 120 men and women were hanged at the prison between 1791
and 1936 for crimes ranging from murder to forgery and for stealing
such items as wheat, horses and cloth. From 1868 the citizens of
Gloucester were denied the spectacle of public executions following
the provision of a purpose-built chamber within the gaol walls.

After the Prison Act of 1877 the buildings passed from the control
of the county magistrates to become H.M. Prison, Gloucester which
was eventually designated an all-male establishment in 1915. Today
the prison accommodates referals from three crown courts and thirty-
seven magistrate courts in the counties of Gloucestershire, Herefordshire and Worcestershire.

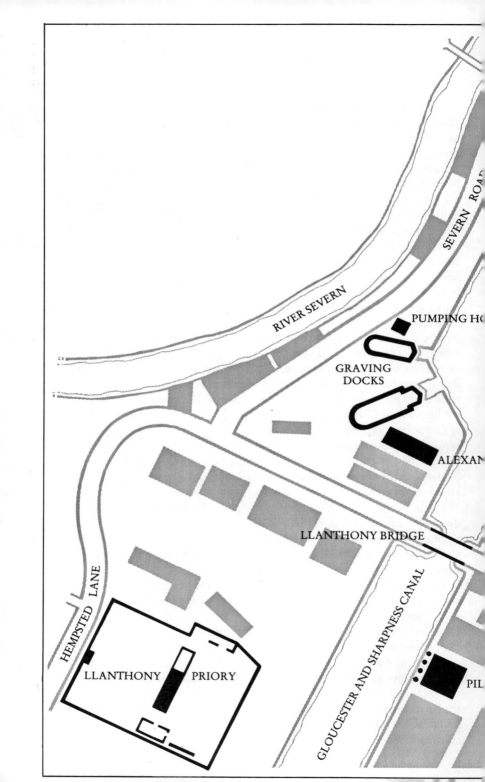

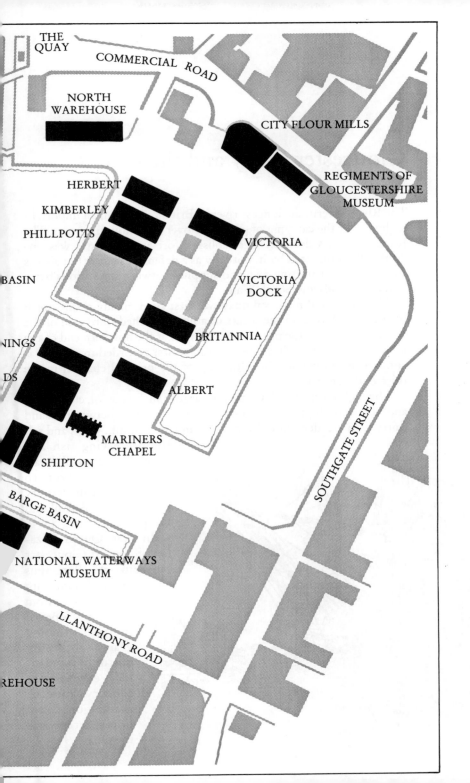

Gloucester Quay and the Docks

The River Severn, the longest river in Britain, has been an important highway for the carrying of goods for over two thousand years. The Roman Army's decision to establish a fort at Gloucester was undoubtedly influenced by it, not only as a defensive feature but also as a means of transporting men and supplies between the various bases in the Midlands and South Wales.

The Saxon and medieval quay was first sited mainly to the north of Westgate Street on the banks of a now vanished third arm of the Severn that joined the present east channel at the northern end of the modern river quay. This later quayside, first recorded in 1390, was constructed following the silting up of the original channel in the thirteenth century.

Throughout the medieval period cargoes such as wool, cloth, corn and iron were shipped out of Gloucester in vessels of between ten and thirty tons' burden; they also brought in sea-coal, silk, wines and salt for preserving fish and meat. These small boats operated up river to Worcester and Shrewsbury and down to Bristol and Chepstow.

In 1580 Queen Elizabeth I granted Gloucester the status of a Port, thus allowing direct trade with foreign ports. A custom house was opened in the following year, probably on the site of the existing eighteenth-century building near the junction of Quay Street and the Quay.

Trade continued to grow during the next two centuries, so much so, that in 1780 over six hundred boats berthed at Gloucester. From 1791 a few vessels brought in cargoes of wine from Spain and Portugal but these larger vessels could only reach the city on the highest spring tides due to the restricted river channels to the south of Gloucester. In consequence most foreign trade was still transhipped at Bristol. In a bid to improve the city's waterborne trade, a proposal was made by leading merchants in Gloucester and the Midlands to construct a canal to Berkeley that would bypass these obstructions and also provide a link with the Stroudwater and Thames and Severn canals thereby opening a direct route between the Midlands and the capital.

The Gloucester and Berkeley Canal

The Act of Parliament for the Gloucester and Berkeley Canal was passed in 1793 and excavation work began the following year. The project soon became dogged by a series of technical and management problems and was further disadvantaged by the severe underestimation of the cost. The original capital investment ran out in 1800 with only eight of the intended 28.5 km. (17¾ miles) having been completed. Work on the canal resumed in 1817 with the aid of government loans under the supervision of Thomas Telford who agreed that the route should be shortened to enter the Severn at Sharpness. The canal was eventually linked with the Stroudwater Canal in 1820 and the whole of the 25.8 km. (16 mile) long waterway between Gloucester and Sharpness was officially opened to traffic in 1827.

The MAIN BASIN was excavated between 1794 and 1797 to a depth of 4.9m. (16 feet) by men using shovels and wheelbarrows. The basin was opened to river traffic in 1812 so that coal from the Forest of Dean could be transferred from boats into the horse-drawn wagons of the Gloucester and Cheltenham Tramroad.

Warehouses

The superb collection of warehouses within the docks owe their existence to the corn trade of the nineteenth century when huge quantities of wheat, oats, barley and maize were shipped into the port from Ireland, North Europe, the Mediterranean and the Black Sea.

Following its arrival in the hold of a tall-masted schooner or barque, the bulk grain was measured into sacks that could hold four bushels. The sack was lifted out of the hold onto the deck for weighing

and topping up if necessary. It was then hoisted from the deck up to
the required floor level of the warehouse by means of a winch operated by two men in the roof. On arrival at the appropriate floor the
114 kg. (2¼ cwt.) sack was swung through the doorway onto a sack
truck or the back of a brawny porter to be carried to the stack. When
required, the grain was lowered onto barges (or later into railway
wagons) for transportation to various parts of the country.

At the northern end of the basin is the North Warehouse, built in
1827 by the Gloucester and Berkeley Canal Company for renting out
to individual corn merchants. The extensive basements were used
initially as bonded stores by local wine and spirit importers. At the

south-east corner of
the building hangs a
bell from the *Atlas* sail-
ing ship that was bro-
ken up in 1832. The
bell was used to regu-
late the starting and
finishing times of the
dock workers until
1941 when it was re-
moved to Sheppardine
on the lower reaches of
the Severn to provide a
navigation aid in fog. It was returned here in 1986 by the Gloucester
Civic Trust and the Rotary Club of Gloucester. The North Warehouse together with the adjacent Herbert, Kimberley and Phillpotts
Warehouses, built in 1846, have been restored by the Gloucester City
Council to provide accommodation for all their administrative offices.
At the eastern end of the North Warehouse is a drinking fountain
provided by the local Board of Health in 1863.

City Flour Mills

Imported wheat was milled in the dock area following the construction of the City Flour Mills by J. & J. Hadley in 1850. Since 1881 these
mills have been operated by the independent firm of Priday Metford
& Co. who supply flour now made from mainly home-grown crops
to many local bakeries.

The Custom House:
The Regiments of Gloucestershire Museum

Adjacent to the flour mills is the Custom House that has a finely
proportioned classical façade overlooking Commercial Road. The
building was opened in 1845 to provide more spacious accommodation in which to deal with the anticipated growth in foreign trade. It
is now occupied by the Regiments of Gloucestershire Museum who
installed a new entrance at the rear of the building in the 1980s to give
access from within the docks, so echoing the famous order 'Rear Rank
28th Right about face' given to the regiment at the Battle of Alexandria
in 1801. For their gallantry in defeating the French, the 28th were
granted the unique distinction of wearing a badge at the back of their
headdress as well as at the front.

The Victoria Dock

The Victoria Dock was opened to water traffic in 1849 due to increased
trade following the repeal of the Corn Laws. This dock also became
known as the Salt Basin for it was here that salt ferried down river from
Stoke Prior and Droitwich was transhipped into schooners and ketches
for export to Ireland and the Continent. The Victoria, Brittania and
Albert Warehouses face onto the basin, with the latter now housing
the nostalgic Robert Opie Museum of Advertising and Packaging.

The Mariners' Chapel

In the first half of the nineteenth century the dock gates were
closed on Sundays, and no cargo handling was allowed. The
sailors' clothes were considered inappropriate for worship
in the city churches which led to the creation of a public
subscription by the docks traders to provide a church
specifically for the crews of the visiting ships. In
1849 the Mariners' Chapel opened and initially
became very fashionable with the townspeople who flocked here in large numbers. The
chaplain in charge was responsible for visiting every ship that arrived in Gloucester to
distribute bibles and religious tracts and for
visiting the two homes for sailors in the city. He
also conducted open air services for the families

who lived aboard the numerous longboats that usually moored in the Barge Basin. This community generally shunned the new chapel because they considered it 'too posh'. Regular services are still held here with a congregation drawn from various parts of the city.

The Vinings and Reynolds Warehouses

The Vinings and Reynolds Warehouses were built in 1840 for the storage of corn. Near the corner of the Barge Basin can be seen a different and earlier form of warehouse built in 1830 for John Biddle, a prominent miller from Stroud; the architectural style is reminiscent of the mills found in that area. Biddle imported grain through Gloucester and transported it in barges to his mills via the Stroud-water Canal. This building, together with the adjacent Shipton Warehouse, was occupied early in the twentieth century by the Severn and Canal Carrying Co. who operated a fleet of boats on the waterways between Gloucester and the Midlands. This corner of the docks is much sought after by film and television companies as an ideal location for period productions that have a maritime theme.

National Waterways Museum

The superb National Waterways Museum occupies several floors of the Llanthony Warehouse, the largest in the Docks, where the rich history of Britain's Inland Water-ways is brought to life by way of imagina-tive displays and a collection of historic and unusual vessels.

From Llanthony Bridge can be seen the northernmost stretch of the Gloucester and Sharpness canal which at the time of construction was the long-est, deepest and broadest ship canal in Britain. The sixteen-mile length is crossed by sixteen bridges that span a waterway six-teen feet deep. On the eastern bank near the bridge is the Pillar Warehouse constructed so as to allow goods to be hoisted directly out of a ship's hold while still retaining a passageway along the quayside.

Most of the eastern bank of the canal as far as Hempsted Bridge was used for the storage of timber imported by local merchants from the Baltic and North America. Due to the dearth of local exports to the American continent most of the visiting ships had to obtain return cargoes from other ports. The timber merchants Price & Company attempted to reverse this situation by filling their ships with parties of emigrants. Many were families from the surrounding towns and villages intent on escaping the economic hardships of the 1850s and, on one voyage, the 250 passengers consisted mainly of young paupers brought from Cheltenham to Gloucester aboard a special train.

On the western bank at the southern end of Llanthony Quay stands the tall form of a grain silo built as a strategic grain store during the Second World War. Immediately to its south is the Monk Meadow dock basin opened in 1892 in response to increased trade. In the 1920s this dock became the centre of oil storage facilities at Gloucester, and oil was also carried up river in petroleum barges to Worcester and Stourport.

Dry Docks

On the western side of the Main Dock basin, near the Alexandra Warehouse are two graving or dry docks. The smaller and earlier of the two was first commissioned in 1818 for repairing vessels trading on the river. The dock was normally drained directly into the river, but when the river level was high manual pumps had to be used taking eight men up to seven hours to pump the dock dry. In 1853 a second graving dock was opened to cater for the larger ships trading at Gloucester.

The high volume of water lost from the canal during the operation of the locks at each end is replenished by feeder streams and by drawing water from the river. Originally this was carried out by steam driven pumps in the engine house near the small dry dock. Today the modern pumping house on the west quay houses an electric centrifugal pump which together with a second pump in the engine house can deliver up to three million gallons of Severn water per hour when required. The water provided by these pumps is also used to augment the public supply to Bristol that is drawn out of the canal at a treatment plant at Purton. The supply from the river contains a high silt content that tends to settle in the Main Basin which, in consequence, has to be dredged regularly. The dredger deposits the silt into a series of barges which are towed down the canal to the south of Purton where the load is pumped back into the river. It has been suggested that this same silt arrives back at Gloucester on the following high tide where it is pumped back into the dock basin!

The water level in the Main Basin is about 3.8m. (12 ft. 6 in.) above the summer level of the River Severn, and the two are linked by a lock 63.4 m. (208 ft.) long by 6.8 m. (22½ ft.) wide that can accommodate vessels up to 400 tons carrying capacity.

Llanthony Priory

In the second decade of the thirteenth century Walter of Gloucester relinquished his posts as Sheriff for the County and Constable of Gloucester castle to his son Miles in order to spend the rest of his days in the peace and tranquility of the Augustinian priory at Llanthony in the Black Mountains of Wales. In 1136 the priory was attacked by Welsh rebels forcing the prior and canons to flee to Gloucester where they received the patronage of Miles who gave them endowments and land to the south of his castle for the building of a new religious house. The church was built within sixteen months and the priory was completed by 1150, just four years before the Welsh house was restored. Llanthony Secunda prospered through the generosity of many burgesses and eminent traders to become a major property owner and patron of three parish churches in the town.

The priory became noted for the lavish hospitality and catering expertise provided by the canons, officers and the servants of the eighty-strong lay community. In the early thirteenth century they undertook the daunting task of providing bread, potage and ale to one thousand poor people twice a year in commemoration of the deaths of two benefactors.

Henry III and his court conducted business of state at the priory in July, 1241, and the widowed Queen Eleanor, living at Gloucester Castle in 1277, was granted permission to walk in the prior's garden. The deposed Edward II lodged at the priory in April 1327 while under escort to Berkeley Castle where he was foully murdered five months later.

The Augustinian house suffered a series of misfortunes in the first half of the fourteenth century, beginning with a disastrous fire in 1301 that destroyed the church and its four bell towers. Controversy raged around the election of priors and the resulting poor management led

to serious financial problems. The ravages of the
Black Death visited the priory in 1349 causing the
deaths of nineteen of the thirty canons in residence.

During the Gloucester Parliament of 1378 the
priory was the setting for the execution of one of
John of Gaunt's stable lads who was accused of
murder and convicted at a special sitting of the
King's Bench.

The duke of Buckingham and his army of two
hundred troops were quartered at Llanthony following unrest in the town in 1381. The national
resentment caused by King Richard's introduc-
tion of the Poll Tax was reflected at Gloucester
where the burgesses expressed their feelings by
dumping large quantities of butchers' offal and
other stinking detritus under the castle walls,
much to the annoyance of the constable. Following a meeting between
the duke and the aggrieved parties the ringleaders were arrested and
imprisoned in the castle gaol.

The most distinguished prior of Llanthony was Henry Dene, a
member of the King's Council, who held the post from 1461 until his
resignation in 1501 when he became archbishop of Canterbury. Dene
initiated major building and restoration works at the priory and
during the latter years of his incumbency combined the various offices
of bishop of Bangor, chancellor of Ireland, deputy governor of Ireland
and bishop of Salisbury.

When the priory was dissolved in 1538 it was amongst the richest
Augustinian houses in England owning 97 churches and 51 manors
in England, Ireland and Wales. The estate was sold to Arthur Porter,
four times MP for the city and county. In 1615 it passed, by marriage,
to viscount Scudamore.

Soon after the outbreak of civil war Scudamore, a royalist sympathiser, was captured and imprisoned after collecting weapons from his
arsenal at Llanthony. In 1643, as the king's army approached
Gloucester, the town clerk ordered the demolition of the priory
church tower to deny the besiegers a useful vantage point. The royalist
General Ruthven built a camp behind the priory and installed a
battery to attack the south-western quadrant of the city.

In 1768 the property passed to Charles Howard, 11th Duke of
Norfolk, who was mayor of Gloucester in 1798, 1809 and 1815. In
1820 the estate passed by way of inheritance to John Higford; to

Daniell Higford Davall Burr MP, and then to John Collett a manufacturing chemist. More recently the principal remains of the priory were purchased from British Rail by the Gloucester City Council in 1974.

The remains of the outer gatehouse, built about 1500, comprise a pedestrian doorway set below the gatekeeper's chamber. The single-light window was originally closed by a wooden shutter and is surrounded by three stone shields. The uppermost one bore the arms of King Henry VII who visited the priory in 1501; on the left are the arms of the Bohun family, benefactors to the priory from 1175 to 1373, and to the right the shield bears a chevron with three Cornish choughs for Henry Dene, Prior of Llanthony and Bishop of Bangor.

The battlemented precinct wall to the south of the gatehouse consists mainly of early sixteenth-century brickwork that contains lozenge-shaped patterning and a two dimensional wayside cross in vitrified headers.

The gateway gives access to the quadrangular outer court of the precincts which housed the bakery, brewery, dairy and other farm buildings that were arranged around the inside of the western and northern precinct walls. The pond was dug in the later nineteenth century to provide water for cattle.

The fifteenth-century tithe barn originally stored the arable crops produced by the Llanthony estate but fell into disuse during the seventeenth century due to a greater emphasis on cattle production.

The range in the centre of the site reached its present form in the late fifteenth century when the close-studded timber-framed upper storey was added to an earlier masonry ground floor. The six surviving bays formed the middle portion of a building that was originally thirty bays long. The first floor of the standing building contained a senior canons' lodging at the southern end and a granary or store in its northern part. The late nineteenth-century farmhouse occupies the site of a gatehouse that gave access to the inner court of the priory.

The priory church and cloister stood on the eastern side of this court but sadly nothing is visible above ground today. Many of the priory's benefactors who were buried in the eastern end of the church were swept from their last resting place during the construction of the Gloucester and Sharpness Canal that sliced through the site at the end of the eighteenth century.

Historical Calendar

c. 49	Fortress established by the Roman army at Kingsholm near the lowest practical crossing of the River Severn.
c. 65	New fortress established on the site of the modern city centre.
c. 96	*Colonia Nerviae Glevensium* founded as a colony for retired Roman soldiers. One of only four in Britain.
577	Battle of Dyrham gave Saxons control of Gloucester, Bath and Cirencester.
679	Foundation of St Peter's Monastery by Osric.
871	Gloucester mint created by Alfred the Great.
877	King Guthrum and his invading Danish army camp here before moving on to take Chippenham.
896	Alfred the Great held his Great Witan at Gloucester.
c. 900	St Oswald's Minster founded by Queen Aethelflaeda.
909	Gloucester refortified by Queen Aethelflaeda against the Danes.
918	Queen Aethelflaeda buried at Gloucester.
931	Priory of Black Canons of St Augustine founded on the site of St John's Church.
940	27 October. King Athelstan, grandson of Alfred the Great, dies at Gloucester.
946	King Edmund passes through Gloucester prior to his death at Pucklechurch.
964	King Edgar holds Witan here.
1016	Edmund 'Ironside' and Cnut, King of Denmark, meet at the Isle of Alney to sign treaty marking the end of war between the English and the Vikings.
1022	St Peter's reformed under Benedictine order.
1043	Edward the Confessor holds the first of many councils at Kingsholm palace.
1066	William of Normandy conquers England and holds his Great Council Meeting at Gloucester.
c. 1068	Norman castle built.
1072	Serlo appointed Abbot of St Peter's.
1085	Domesday book ordered by William the Conqueror during the Christmas parliament at Gloucester.
1086	William holds his last court at Gloucester.

1088	St Peter's Abbey burned down.
1089	29 June. Serlo lays foundation stone of present cathedral building. 11 August. Earthquake felt in city.
1093	William II falls ill at Gloucester. King Malcolm, refused an audience, returns to Scotland to prepare to invade England.
1094	William II at his Christmas court orders the invasion of Normandy against his older brother Robert Curthose.
1100	A Gloucester monk foretells the violent death of William II.
1102	Thursday 22 May. Great fire burns St Peter's Church and the city.
c. 1110	Medieval castle built on the banks of the Severn.
1122	Wednesday 8 March. Lightning striking the steeple causes fire at St Peter's Abbey.
1123	New Archbishop of Canterbury chosen at Gloucester.
1134	Robert Curtehose, son of William the Conqueror, buried at St Peter's church, at his own request.
1137	Priory church of Llanthony Secunda consecrated.
1141	Earliest record of a church at St Mary de Crypt. King Stephen captured at the Battle of Lincoln is imprisoned at Gloucester castle.
c. 1142	Henry Plantaganet resides in Gloucester between the ages of nine and fourteen. He returns a few years later to discover 'fair Rosamunde' at nearby Frampton on Severn.
1150	Llanthony Priory completed.
1155	Henry II gives charter to Gloucester allowing the same privileges as those of London and Westminster.
1168	Jewish community accused of murdering a young Christian boy.
1188	John, younger son of Henry II courts Hadwisa, daughter of Earl William of Gloucester.
1190	11 May. Great fire burned down most of the town including St Mary de Lode and St Oswald's.
1200	King John, at Gloucester, gives safe conduct to William, King of Scotland.
1210	River Severn freezes to four miles above Gloucester.
1214	Town severely damaged by fire
1216	28 October. Henry III crowned at St Peter's Abbey.
1222	A great fire consumes Lower Westgate Street area.
1223	Fire consumes both sides of Upper Westgate Street down to College Street.
1231	Foundation of Greyfriars.
1233	22 May. Henry III holds Parliament here.
1234	29 May. Parliament held at Gloucester.

c. 1239	Foundation of Blackfriars.
1241	July. Henry III conducts Business of State at Llanthony Priory.
1263	Henry III imprisoned at Gloucester Castle during the Barons War. Prince Edward delivers the city from the hands of Simon de Montfort.
1275	Jewish community expelled from Gloucester by Queen Eleanor.
1277	Queen Eleanor resides at Gloucester Castle.
1278	Edward I holds Parliament here and enacts the 'Statute of Gloucester'.
1287	Edward I holds Parliament here.
1300	Third fire to damage Abbey buildings.
1301	Llanthony Priory church gutted by fire.
1320-26	Edward II visits Gloucester on numerous occasions.
1326	Edward II flees to Wales via Gloucester from his wife Isabella and her invading French allies.
1327	Edward II murdered at Berkeley Castle and buried at St Peter's Abbey in the presence of Edward III.
1337	10 October. Edward III visits.
1349	Black Death plague arrives in town.
1378	Richard II summons Parliament at St Peter's Abbey.
1390	Richard II in the town after reports of miracles at Edward II's tomb.
1407	20 October. Whilst holding Parliament here Henry IV paved the way for bringing public finances under parliamentary control.
1420	Henry V holds Parliament here.
1430-50	New Inn built under the direction of John Twyning, the Town Monk.
1471	Queen Margaret and her army denied passage through the city to join forces in Wales. Edward IV was received on his way to defeating her at the Battle of Tewkesbury.
1483	6 July. Richard, Duke of Gloucester, is crowned king. 2 September. Richard III visits Gloucester and grants Letters Patent giving Gloucester the right to self-government.
1485	Refugees from the Battle of Bosworth seek refuge in St John's Church following the slaying of Richard III, Duke of Gloucester. Henry VII visits Gloucester.
c. 1500	Fleece Hotel built by St Peter's Abbey.
1535	31 July. Henry VIII and Anne Boleyn visit.
1536	Following the Dissolution of Monasteries Blackfriars is sold to Thomas Bell for £250 5s. 4d.
1538	Tudor Coat of Arms granted.
1539	Crypt Grammar school founded.

1553   Accession of Mary Tudor proclaimed from the New Inn.

1555   9 February. Bishop John Hooper burned at the stake in St Mary's Square.

1574   8 August. Royal progress of Elizabeth I arrives at Gloucester.

1575   Earthquake damage to city.

1580   Queen Elizabeth I at Gloucester grants the city Port status.
          24 August. John Taylor, water poet, born here.

1592   Whilst residing at Sudeley Castle Elizabeth again visits Gloucester.

1604   City population decimated by plague.

1642   Outbreak of the English Civil War.

1643   10 August. King Charles I beseiges the city after being refused entry. He and his sons reside at Matson House.
          5 September. City relieved by Earl of Essex and his London army.

1654   First HMS *Gloucester* is launched.

1661   Charles II orders destruction of city's defences.

1666   Blue Coat School founded by Sir Thomas Rich.

1687   August. James II makes Royal Progress to the city.

1714   16 December. George Whitefield born at the Bell Inn.

1716   Earliest known bank in Gloucester opened by a local merchant.

1722   9 April. First publication of the *Gloucester Journal* by Robert Raikes.

1736   Birth of Robert Raikes junior, pioneer of Sunday Schools.

1750   John Stafford Smith born here.

1751   High Cross taken down in a street clearance scheme.

1755   Gloucester Infirmary opened.

1781   Act of Parliament allows the demolition of the North, Outer North and South gates.

1788   July. George III made three visits with Queen Charlotte and children.

1791   County Gaol opened.

1801   Battle of Alexandra where the Gloucestershire Regiment, or 28th, were granted the distinction of wearing a badge at the back of the headress as well as the front.

1802   Sir Charles Wheatstone born in Westgate Street.

1803   Thomas Stock, joint pioneer of Sunday School Movement, dies.

1807   5 October. George, Prince Regent, accepts the Freedom of the City and dines with the corporation at the King's Head, Westgate Street.

1818   First graving dock commissioned at Gloucester Docks.

1827   Gloucester and Sharpness Canal opened to traffic.

1849   29 September. Queen Victoria visits Gloucester and is offered a carpet for her personal use. She later gave permission for its sale to the public.

W. E. Henley born in Eastgate Street.

1852   30 August. Gloucester station is decorated for Queen Victoria when she changed trains here due to the difference in the gauge of track between the Midland and Great Western Railway Companies.

1890   Ivor Gurney born in Queen Street.

1909   23 June. Edward, Prince of Wales, visits the Royal Agriculture Society's Show on the Oxleaze. He granted the title 'Royal' to the Infirmary, Southgate Street.

1912   City Fire Brigade created.

1940   February. King George VI and Queen Elizabeth visit Gloster Aircraft Company, Hucclecote, to inspect the construction of fighter aircraft.

1955   3 May. Queen Elizabeth II and Prince Philip's visit celebrates the 800th anniversary of Henry II's charter of 1155.

1979   HRH Princess Anne re-opens Ladybellegate House after its refurbishment by Gloucester Civic Trust.

1980   21 June. Duke of Gloucester officially opens 'Port 400' celebrations.

1982   Tenth HMS *Gloucester* launched.

1987   City Council Headquarters moved from the Guildhall to the refurbished North Warehouse at the Docks.

1986   14 April. Queen Elizabeth II opens the new Widden Street Primary School.

1990   6 November. HRH Prince of Wales' visit.

Museums and Art Galleries

Opening Times

Gloucester City Museum and Art Gallery, Brunswick Road.
  Monday–Saturday 10.00–17.00 including Bank Holiday Mondays.
  Sundays 10.00–16.00 July to September only.

Gloucester Folk Museum, 99–103 Westgate Street.
  Monday–Saturday 10.00–17.00 including Bank Holiday Mondays.
  Sundays 10.00–16.00 July to September only.

The National Waterways Museum, The Docks.
  Daily 10.00–18.00 Summer; 10.00–17.00 Winter.
  Closed Christmas Day.

Regiments of Gloucestershire Museum, The Docks.
  Tuesday–Sunday and Bank Holidays 10.00–17.00.

Robert Opie Collection – Museum of Advertising and Packaging, The Docks.
  Daily 10.00–18.00 May–September.
  Tuesday–Sunday 10.00–17.00 October–April.
  Open on all Bank Holidays except Christmas Day and Boxing Day.

House of the Tailor of Gloucester, 9 College Court.
  Monday–Saturday 09.30–17.30.
  Closed Bank Holiday.

The East Gate of Gloucester, Eastgate Street.
  Wednesdays and Fridays 14.15–17.00 May–September
  Saturdays 10.00–12.00, 14.15–17.00.

Gloucester Tourist Information Centre, St Michael's Tower, The Cross.
  Telephone (0452) 421188.
  Monday–Saturday 10.00–17.00.

Tourist Information Point, National Waterways Museum, The Docks.
  Daily 10.00–18.00 Summer; 10.00–17.00 Winter.
  Closed Christmas Day and Boxing Day.

Index